Lorri

Praise for *Creating*

'As creatively encouraging as The Artist's Way – truly helpful for anyone who wants to dream big and live life to the full!'
SHAMA HYDER, CEO, Zen Marketing

'When Michael first shared the principles behind creating the impossible with me, I was rather skeptical. They seemed too simple and too good to be true. However, since that time, I have become even happier in myself and more successful. I recommend you try it as well.'
PAUL McKENNA, D. Phil., #1 international best-selling author and television personality

'This book was written for anyone who wants to cut through the noise of their daily lives to get to the heart of what matters to us all, living a fulfilling life. Nothing less. The process Michael lays out makes self-realization a step-by-step attainable goal.'
SOPHIE CHICHE, founder and CEO of Shape House

'Thoughtful, spontaneous, inspired, lofty, down to earth, and with the clarity and good humor to make it highly usable.'
MIKE DOOLEY, *NY Times* best-selling author of *Infinite Possibilities*

'If you're ready to tap into the infinite power that is within you and truly see what is POSSIBLE, this is the book for you. In a fun and practical way Michael will be your coach and guide as you take on the impossible. Take a leap of trust today and prepare to be amazed at the results.'
IYANLA VANZANT, #1 *NY Times* best-selling author and television personality

'A gifted and inspired writer, Michael Neill takes you on a highly motivational journey that stimulates the creative process from within. Thought provoking and powerful principles are contained on every page of this book, and by aligning yourself with them you can overcome obstacles and manifest your dreams on the path to a more fulfilling life.'

ANITA MOORJANI, *NY Times* best-selling author of *Dying to Be Me* and *What If This Is Heaven?*

'Michael Neill's Creating the Impossible *liberates us from limitations and ignites the fire of creativity that yearns to find free expression in, as, and through us. Whatever your dream, this book will be your trustworthy guide for cultivating the creative courage to bring it into manifestation.'*

MICHAEL BERNARD BECKWITH, author of *Spiritual Liberation* and *Life Visioning*

'I have always thought that success happens when one's inner drive is bigger than the person doing the driving. There are always obstacles along the way that need to be overcome, and unless there is a real passion it's just too easy to quit. And this is what I love about this book. It's all about finding that inner drive and spinning it into forward motion. Michael Neill has a highly infectious and inspiring way of laying out how you can reach your "impossible" goal using practical strategies. I can't think of a more inspiring and useful book to get your wheels spinning forward and achieving your limitless goals.'

CHRIS STANDRING, #1 billboard chart-topping jazz-recording artist

'After a career of working with highly creative people, I found Michael Neill's approach to be very insightful. Michael stays away from the buzz words and easy bromides that I anticipated and instead delivers a new and easy-to-comprehend method of attacking the dreaded blank page of the creative process. I flagged more than a few pages for myself to review again.'

MICHAEL WOLF, award-winning animation producer of *The Simpsons*, *Family Guy*, and *King of the Hill*

'Michael Neill is an indisputable genius, and Creating the Impossible *is a thoughtful yet practical guide to creating the life you desire. Use this book to explore new ideas and philosophies and then follow the 90-day plan to bring your dreams into reality.*'

AJIT NAWALKHA, CEO, Evercoach and Co-founder, Mindvalley

'We have seen Michael Neill continually build, create, and re-imagine his life and his dreams, while also helping thousands of people to do the same. He's naturally lived through all the days outlined in this book himself, and there is no better person to write a book about how that same potential of the mind lies within all of us. We are continually dumbfounded by how fast, fun, and possible the game of creation is when you understand what Michael is pointing to in these pages, and this book will show you how true that really is.'

EIRIK GRUNDE OLSEN and MARA GLEASON OLSEN,
co-founders of the One Solution Global Initiative

'Impossible is just a thought, and Michael Neill's latest book is a beautiful brainstorm of possibilities for all of us who want to create an artful life. Very highly recommended!'

STEVE CHANDLER, best-selling author of *Time Warrior* and *101 Ways to Motivate Yourself*

'Michael has a charming gift that lets you easily understand and personally experience both the "putting it into action" and "then a miracle happens" parts of your creative process. A wonderful read!'

DR. THOMAS GARTENMANN, Managing Partner,
aergon inside-out leadership transformation, Zurich, Munich

'Michael Neill does it yet again! His 90-day program is a super-easy, straightforward, no-nonsense guide to get you taking action on your biggest goals with ease. The way he weaves simplicity into breaking down your fears to seize hold on your greatest achievements is organized, brilliant, and relatable. A must for any game-changer, entrepreneur, or change agent!'

DR. NEETA BHOUSHAN, best-selling author and executive coach

CREATING
— THE —
IMPOSSIBLE

A 90-DAY PROGRAM TO GET YOUR DREAMS
OUT OF YOUR HEAD AND INTO THE WORLD

MICHAEL NEILL

HAY HOUSE

Carlsbad, California • New York City • London
Sydney • Johannesburg • Vancouver • New Delhi

Published and distributed in the United States by: Hay House, Inc.: www
.hayhouse.com® • *Published and distributed in Australia by*: Hay House
Australia Pty. Ltd.: www.hayhouse.com.au • *Published and distributed in the
United Kingdom by*: Hay House UK, Ltd.: www.hayhouse.co.uk • *Distributed
in Canada by*: Raincoast Books: www.raincoast.com • *Published in India by*:
Hay House Publishers India: www.hayhouse.co.in

Cover design: Randy Stuart • *Interior design:* Leanne Siu Anastasi
Interior illustrations: pp. 1, 49 Randy Stuart; all other images Michael Neill

Library of Congress Control Number: 2017948503

Tradepaper ISBN: 978-1-4019-5057-6

10 9 8 7 6 5 4 3 2
1st edition, January 2018

Printed in the United States of America

SUSTAINABLE
FORESTRY
INITIATIVE

Certified Sourcing
www.sfiprogram.org
SFI-01268

SFI label applies to text stock only

To Michael, aged 17.
Here's the book I wish we could have read back then...

All men dream: but not equally. Those who dream by night in the dusty recesses of their mind wake in the day to find that it was vanity. But the dreamers of the day are dangerous men, for they may act their dream with open eyes, to make it possible.

T.E. LAWRENCE, aka LAWRENCE OF ARABIA

Contents

Introduction
What's Your Impossible Dream?

What's the craziest, most outlandishly wonderful thing you can imagine doing over the year ahead? Is it starting a new business? Paying off your debts? Traveling the world? Do you want to write a book, sell your screenplay, or show your art in a gallery? Maybe you want to knock off one of your perpetual New Year's resolutions and learn Italian, run a marathon, or finally fit into that dress you've been keeping in your closet. Or do you long for something even more ambitious – to become a leader in your field, meet and marry your one true love, add a couple of zeros to your income, and make a significant difference in the world?

If these dreams sound ridiculous, or even impossible, good. In fact, that's kind of the point...

Over the past seven years, thousands of people have joined me for an online adventure I call 'Creating the Impossible.' I encourage participants to choose something they want to create that's far beyond their current sense of what's possible. By the time the program is complete, they've often met or exceeded their own expectations of how much can be created in a limited amount of time. They've created new jobs, new relationships, and new income. They've lost weight, started companies, invented products, left bad situations, broken habits, gotten married, and moved on with their lives in ways they hadn't thought possible. More importantly, they've unleashed something fundamental inside themselves and learned to live their lives with an ever-expanding sense of possibility.

How have they done it? They've come to understand a simple truth about the mind that we'll explore together throughout this book – what

I call 'the inside-out understanding' – and woken up to a deeper part of themselves – their innate health, creativity, and resilience.

For the past 40 years or so, people have been using this knowledge to create results that seemed impossible and foolhardy to even contemplate:

- A couple met, fell in love, and now travel the world as the leaders of a non-profit organization, sharing what they see as the one solution to all global problems (*pp.83–84*).

- A project team from a software company took a year off and started a clothing line (*pp.193–95*).

- An aerospace company cut the production time on an 18-month military project in half without increasing the budget or giving their employees heart attacks along the way (*pp.205–206*).

- A biotech company found an extra US$200 million in earnings during a three-day exploration of how the mind worked (*pp.209–210*).

Now it's your turn!

In the first part of this book, 'Making the Invisible Visible,' I'll guide you through the creative process and introduce you to the principles behind the inside-out understanding. You'll gain a new appreciation for how the mind works that will make it easier than ever for you to navigate the highs and lows of daily life while creating inspired and inspiring results in the world. I'll illustrate the secrets of effortless (and exponential) productivity and share the formula for creating that I've taught to nearly all my corporate and individual clients over the years – a simple two-step process that makes creating pretty much anything a straightforward proposition.

Then in the second part, 'Making the Impossible Possible,' I'll coach you through a 90-day program that will help you get your own impossible dreams out of your head and into the world. The only things you'll need to bring to the table are something you'd love to create and a willingness to change your mind once and for all about what's truly possible in your world.

How to Get the Most Out of This Book

I've been working with high performers for over 25 years. One of my more memorable teaching experiences came a few years back when I was facilitating a group of coaches in New York City and someone asked a question about 'the limits of human creativity.'

After letting the conversation run for a bit, I jumped in and pointed out that while the creative output of any individual would inherently be limited, the source and fundamental principles behind that creativity and the source of our own creative power were unlimited.

I got on a bit of a roll, as I am sometimes wont to do, and before I stepped back off my soapbox I completed my rant with a line that my then 16-year-old daughter immortalized by tweeting it out from the back of the room:

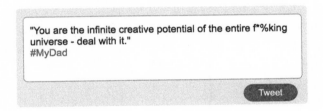

"You are the infinite creative potential of the entire f*%king universe - deal with it."
#MyDad

Tweet

The premise behind this book is the same as the one I shared on that day:

There is an innate creative energy in all of us. It's the animating spirit that separates the quick from the dead – the life-force that expands our lungs, makes our heart beat, and takes care of every one of our biological functions. If we let it, it will bring fresh new ideas to mind whenever we need them, enabling us to solve any problem and move forward in any creative endeavor.

Our relationship with this energy is the basis of what we call 'creativity.' And since this energy is a part of us and we are a part of it, we are all inherently creative.

So, while this is a book about how things are created, it's also a book about how we can find our role in their creation and embrace that role more fully.

Here are a few pointers to help you get the most out of yourself and this book as you read on:

1. Read for insight, not information

I once met a guy who moved from Los Angeles to New York City after the big Northridge earthquake in 1994 destroyed the apartment building in which he was living. Short on cash but determined to make a fresh start as far away from 'earthquake country' as he could get, he moved into a tiny apartment in the Bronx.

His first night in the new building, he woke up at 5 a.m. to feel the floor underneath his bed shaking. Horrified that he had somehow managed to be a part of the first recorded earthquake in New York history, he sat down at his kitchen table to catch his breath and consider his options.

Then at 5:30 a.m. the floor started to shake again. Obviously it was an aftershock from the original quake. Another came at 5:45 a.m. And another at 6 a.m.

The fourth time it happened, it dawned on the man that what he was feeling wasn't an earthquake. It was the subway running underneath the apartment building.

Although the apartment kept on shaking, after having that realization, he never worried about it again.

In the same way, what impacts us most isn't *information* (like knowing there are no earthquakes in New York City), it's *insight* – the realization of something that's always been true, regardless of what we happen to believe.

So my suggestion is that as best you can, read through each chapter in the book the way you might read a thriller or some light beach reading. Enjoy it, savor it even, but don't think you need to take notes or remember everything word for word.

2. Look for principles, not strategies

Most books on creativity, goal-setting, productivity, and performance are packed with 'how to' strategies designed to be followed step by step. Will following those steps take you where you want to go? Unfortunately, that's the exception, not the rule. True creativity is an individual and in the moment process, and there are no guarantees when it comes to results.

However, there are iron-clad principles that we can rely on no matter what. These invisible forces are at work in the world whether we know about them or not. They are as practical as electricity, as powerful as gravity, and as mysterious as magnetism. They make sense of everything we do (or don't do) with our life and time.

Which is why when it comes to creating, instead of looking for *strategies*, I encourage you first to seek to understand the *principles* of creation – not how to do it, but how it actually works. Then you'll know what to do whatever the situation. And as your insight into the principles behind creation deepens, you'll find the game of creating gets simpler and more enjoyable to play.

How do I do it?	How does it work?
strategies	principles
engineering	physics
variable	constant
personal	universal
prescriptive	descriptive
useful ways of thinking about things	true whether we believe it or not

3. Be an explorer, not a researcher

In talking with thousands of people about these principles over the past number of years, I've noticed a very distinct difference between people who come to them as though they're studying for an exam and those who are listening to be impacted by what they hear. And what I've realized is that it's what you actually see for yourself that matters, not what you can repeat when asked.

I think of this as the difference between 'researching' and 'exploring.' When we 'research,' we're collecting data samples, making comparisons, and drawing conclusions. When we're genuinely exploring, we come to the conversation with an open mind, ready and willing to throw ourselves into the unknown and see whatever is there for us to see. Instead of listening for 'the right answer,' we look to see what's true.

When it comes to creating the impossible, there's no final exam – there's just your dreams and your life. And there are only three ways we can fail to bring our dreams to life, no matter how impossible they may seem:

- We don't start because we think that it's futile, pointless, too late, and we're not the right person to do it anyway, and those thoughts seem real and true to us.

- We stop because our head is filled with thoughts telling us that we've left it too late, we're not having fun, it's too hard, and it's not going to happen anyway.

- We run out of time because we made up a time-frame that was too short for the project at hand or because we were handed a time-frame and, for whatever reason, things just didn't happen in that time.

In other words, we *think* our way in and out of action all day long. But the wonderful thing about our thoughts is that they're just thoughts – no more solid than clouds and no more powerful than the power we give them.

So, no matter what you find yourself thinking as we explore your creative potential together, the best advice I can give you is simply this:

Don't believe everything you think.

Are you ready to begin?

MAKING THE
INVISIBLE VISIBLE

'*What is essential is invisible to the eye.*'
ANTOINE DE SAINT-EXUPÉRY

Chapter 1
The Source of Creativity

*'Writing is an exploration. You start from nothing
and learn as you go... It's like driving a car at
night. You never see further than your headlights,
but you can make the whole trip that way.'*
E.L. Doctorow

A project team sits around a small table in a conference room. At first it seems as though they are getting somewhere – the brainstorming session is animated and the people are enthusiastic. But as time goes on, the fun seems forced and the ideas stop flowing. The room grows quieter, the ideas less frequent.

After a couple of minutes of relative quiet, someone shares a completely new idea, seemingly disconnected from all the previous ones.

It sparks a response, and then another, and within the hour the team has a plan of action for the week ahead.

Where did the new idea come from?

~

The woman has been trying to lose weight for as long as she can remember, even back when she was objectively thin. The voice in her head is relentless as she sits in the park and picks at yet another lettuce leaf, conveniently packaged in a plastic container that she wishes contained pretty much any other kind of food in the world.

She is oblivious to the world around her until she hears a dog barking nearby. She looks up and notices that she is surrounded by grass and trees and animals and beauty. She smiles for the first time in a while and it occurs to her that she's been eating lettuce to punish herself for something mean a 'friend' said about her weight when she was a teenager.

For the first time in a long time, she feels free of the need to give form to her self-hate in the shape of a lettuce leaf.

One month later, she's startled to see that she's lost 12 pounds without dieting and, more importantly, without suffering.

Where did the realization come from?

~

A writer sits in front of his computer, his cursor flashing on the blank page. His hands begin to type. Words appear on the screen without any conscious thought on his part, as if they've somehow traveled through his fingers onto the page.

Where did the words come from?

For thousands of years, people have been trying to understand the source of creativity – the spark of life that brings ideas to mind and allows us to launch those ideas into the world. In ancient Greece, that creative force was personified as the nine muses, daughters of the Greek god Zeus and his lover Mnemosyne, who was herself the personification of memory. Early Christian teachings, on the other hand, suggested that only God himself could create. That form of creation was called *ex nihilo* – creating 'from nothing.'

And this is at the heart of every creative endeavor. Whatever we call it and what or whomever we attribute it to, there is one fundamental truth behind creation:

Everything comes from nothing.

'Nothing,' in this sense, is an almost imperceptible abbreviation of the space of 'no thing' – a way of describing the formless creative energy of the universe before any 'thing' has been created with it. It's the as yet unformed lump of clay, the play dough of possibility out of which everything will be made before it is unmade again and goes back into its container to stay fresh for next time. It exists in stark contrast to 'the little nothing' of our own thoughts, filled with the content of our own already formed hopes, fears, judgments, and recriminations.

What that means is that any time we want to create something truly new and fresh in the world, we must go beyond the noise of our own mind and into the quiet of the fertile void out of which all things come into being. We need to find the silence beneath the notes, the page beneath the writing, and the space into which our thoughts appear and dissipate.

That space is closer than we think, and larger than our little brain (well, my little brain) can imagine. It's a Big Nothing. We won't find anything when we get there – that's just the nature of nothing – but it is a space of pure potential, an unplowed field so fertile that we need only drop the seed of an idea into it and it will spring to life and begin to grow almost immediately.

We can't see it, but we can get a feel for it. We can touch it by letting it touch us, letting it gently cocoon us in a blanket of life and possibility. It is whispering inspiration into our ear even now.

And while staring into the fertile void can be almost hypnotic, at a certain point we wake up from its depths and feel the impulse to create.

Understanding the Creative Process

How do you get from feeling the creative spark to actually holding something in your hands or seeing it in your life?

Well, if the Big Nothing were a pick-up bar where you ogled potential partners, mucking about with a creative idea would be how you began to flirt with the actual process of bringing something new into the world.

So, if you were drawing, you might start doodling. If you were writing a screenplay, you might begin imagining scenes in your mind. If you were writing a song, you might just start making some noise. If your project were business related, you might start sketching out ideas and daydreaming about people you could enroll in the game.

This is the jumping-off point for the creative process. Just being in motion is enough to make things happen. It's like pushing a stalled car downhill to get the engine started – sometimes we just have to take action in order for our creative engine to catch.

When we're mucking about like this, there's no sense that we're going to use or even keep anything that we do, but we might. We might not. We aren't stuck with it – we're free to take it or leave it. And the more freedom we give ourselves to muck about, the more fun the mucking about is, and the more it tends to lead to inspired action.

And at a certain point, we just kind of know what we're doing, and then we buckle down and do the work. We've hung out at the bar, we've spent time flirting, and now we're going to go on some dates and see what happens. If we're writing, we just need to write. If we're running code, we just need to run code. If we're making calls, we just need to make calls.

This is 'the bit in the middle' – the bit between getting an idea for a great new song and winning a Grammy, between seeing someone we fancy and having grandchildren, and between embarking on any new endeavor and enjoying the fruits of our labors.

This bit in the middle will take some time. It may go on for hours or days or weeks or months or even years, depending on the size and scope of the project. And it may not always be easy. Victor Hugo, the 19th-century author of *Les Misérables* and *The Hunchback of Notre Dame*, struggled so hard to get words out of his head and onto the page that in order to motivate himself, he instructed his servant to lock him naked inside the bathroom each morning with nothing but a candle, quill, ink, and paper. When he had 'darkened the page' sufficiently to pass three pages of writing underneath the bathroom door, his servant would let him out and help him to dress and begin the day.

This is the time when numerous would-be creators give up, assuming that if famous bands can write famous songs in less than an hour, taking more than a week to write the next great novel or more than a year to see a business idea prove successful must mean that they're not really cut out for this kind of thing or they're on the wrong track. All it really means, though, is that they've reached the 'just get on with it' part of the process.

Admittedly, this is in some ways the least sexy part of creating. It's Thomas Edison's 99 percent perspiration that follows the 1 percent inspiration. It's Elvis Presley's TCOB – 'Taking care of business, just as fast as I can.' It's the Nike stage, where you 'just do it.'

If we're not expecting it, we can lose heart. It's a lot grittier and less seemingly magical than other stages. But if you understand that it's just part of the process, then it can become a very rewarding part of the process. For some people, it's the most satisfying part, as it's the most tangible. Everybody can see that you're actually up to something, including you.

How you approach this is up to you. Some people wake up at 2 a.m. on holiday with an idea for a new business and start outlining a five-year plan. Others leave everything until the last minute so they can have the thrill of scrambling to meet a deadline. But whether fast or slow, disciplined or eclectic, inspired by love and passion or fueled by drugs, alcohol, or the need to pay the rent, everyone I've ever met with a high creative output has figured out somewhere along the line that the best way to do good work is to do lots of it. And if you really want to create, at some point you're going to have to do what creators do – show up each day to your keyboard, easel, workbench, or boardroom and put in the hours.

And then at a certain point, doing the work transitions seamlessly into a full-blown experience of creative flow, like a beautiful dance where it's difficult to know who's leading and who's following. We find ourselves in the zone and then step out of our office or studio, and our partners and kids say, 'Where have you been? You missed lunch.' And we think, *Is that the time? I had no idea.*

The flow phase of the creative process is filled with actual miracles and the joy of watching something new come into the world that didn't exist before. And riding the wave of creative flow is a pleasure unlike nearly any other I have known in my 50 years on the planet.

In this state, creating seems effortless. Ideas come to us and through us. Books write themselves, paintings paint themselves, products sell themselves. The hardest part of the process is keeping up and not getting in the way.

But at a certain point we find we are approaching the finish line, that point where we need to let our creation stand on its own two feet, leave home without us and go out into the world. We may still want to run after it to protect and defend it, and yet we know it will either stand or fall by itself.

By way of example, my wife and I love to watch cooking competition shows like *The Great British Bake Off*. There's always that great bit when they do the final countdown: 'Ten, nine, eight…' and everyone is rushing to put the last little bits on their cake and then '…three, two, one, step away!' And they have to step away from their cake, or all their work up to that point will have been in vain.

And that's the final part of the creative process. You step away from your cake, either because someone has told you to or you've decided to, and you … are … done.

How do you know your creation is complete? When you let it go. When you mail it to an agent, post it online, or ship it to your customers. When you lift the lid off the silver platter and say, 'Ta daa!'

In some formal systems of project management they talk about this phase as 'meeting your conditions of satisfaction.' It's a pre-determined point at which a documented list of every expectation required to meet 'success' in a project has been met and signed off on by every stakeholder.

While that can be useful when there are multiple people involved in a creation, it's always seemed a bit more complicated to me than it needs to be. I would say that a simpler rule of thumb is:

You're done when you say that you're done.

Putting It All Together

I began writing what is now the *Caffeine for the Soul* blog when I moved to America at the start of the new millennium. Over 1,000 blog posts later,

I've realized the reason I so love that format as an outlet for the creative energy is that I get to experience the whole of the creative process from start to finish every time I write.

I begin each week with a blank Word document and I muck about until a creative spark catches my imagination – a title, a story, a metaphor, or a snippet of a conversation I've had with a client or friend. At some point a theme emerges and I begin to darken the page, piling word upon word, idea upon idea, paragraph upon paragraph. Sometimes I love the process and get lost in the flow; other times it feels like a chore from start to finish. But by the time I'm done, something exists in the world that didn't exist when I began. It's about as primordial an experience as you can have with a laptop and a good cup of coffee.

Now that may sound a bit grand when all you're creating is a blog post, or a dinner, or a birthday greeting for a friend, but the truth is, creating something from nothing is positively biblical in its implications. In the beginning, there was a word, or a recipe, or a piece of card stock and some glitter. Then you bring something new into the world and either see that it is good and name it to share it with others or destroy it in a flood of self-recrimination and self-loathing. Regardless, when your thought storm passes, you go back to the drawing board and begin again.

Here's a simple experiment that will help you get a feel for the universal creative process at a deeper level:

Before you move on to the next chapter, take some time to create something from nothing – to bring something into the world that doesn't exist right now, except perhaps in its constituent parts. It can be as basic as a paper airplane, as personal as a poem, or as delicious as a three-course meal.

The only requirement is that right now it doesn't exist in the world, and when you're done, it will.

Some Final Thoughts...

As you begin to notice that the phases of the creative journey are always the same, from nothing to something, impulse to action, project to product, you come to see the only real obstacles to creating are how easy it is not to begin and how easy it is not to finish. So in the next chapter, we'll be exploring the constant variable that either holds us back or launches us forward in any creative endeavor.

First, here are a few key points from this chapter for you to reflect on:

- Everything comes from nothing. Therefore the blank page and the creative spark are the birthplace of every creative endeavor.

- When in doubt, begin.

- Putting in the hours and doing the work are the unsung heroes of the creative process.

- You haven't actually created anything until it stands on its own two feet in the world — up to then you've just been busy.

- You're done when you say that you're done.

- The creative process will always involve a journey from nothing to something by way of mucking about, doing the work, riding the flow, and declaring completion.

Chapter 2
The Constant Variable

'The noblest pleasure is the joy of understanding.'
LEONARDO DA VINCI

Francine came to me for coaching on growing her new business. She felt she needed to get better at networking in order to get clients, but, as she told me in no uncertain terms, 'I hate networking. It's fake, and it's phony, and it's just a bunch of people pretending to be interested in someone so they can make money from them.'

When I gently pointed out that it wasn't surprising that someone who thought networking was evil wasn't terribly good at it, she upped the stakes by making her preference a character issue.

'I'm just not the kind of person who can lie, even when it would be in my own best interests. I've tried to fake being interested in people in the past, but it's just not me!'

While the amateur psychologist in me wanted to dive into the content of pretty much everything she said, the professional coach in me knew that the solution wasn't in the specifics of her thinking, but in her misunderstanding of how thought worked.

Thought is the paint with which our reality is created. We think and speak that paint onto the canvas of our consciousness and then experience the painting as if it's real. But no matter how many times we've painted the same picture, it's still just one of a million possible pictures that could be painted on

> **that blank canvas. And no matter how 'photo-realistic' our**
> **preferences are, they're still made up and painted by us.**
> **They're a representation of a possible reality – one tiny sliver**
> **of an infinite creative potential.**

So I told Francine the story of when the abstract painter Pablo Picasso was traveling on a train with a wealthy businessman who criticized his art as being 'unrealistic.' When Picasso asked him to explain, the businessman took a photograph of his wife from his wallet. 'This is my wife, as she is!' he exclaimed.

Picasso examined the photograph and then commented wryly: 'She's very small, your wife. And a bit flat.'

We think we know what things are really like, but we only know what we think. And the wonderful thing about thought is that it can change in the blink of an eye.

The Three Principles

For many years, the human mind has been compared to a computer. The general assumption has been that while some people's computers are more powerful than others (higher IQ, etc.), the main difference between people is in the software – the programs that they run. These programs include both the 'apps,' or strategies, they use, and the 'deeper programs' – their beliefs and values.

Some apps are so popular that we think of them as factory-installed. In the same way that eight out of 10 computers in use today have some version of Microsoft Office installed, so eight out of 10 people will have taken on the majority of the beliefs and values of the culture in which they live.

But far more important to the effectiveness of a computer is what's baked into the firmware – the BIOS (basic input/output system). Even the most effective programs can't run without interfacing with the BIOS of the computer.

The simplest articulation I've come across of the factory-preset human operating system came from Syd Banks, a Scottish welder who had an epiphany at the age of 43 and saw, over the space of a few days, that thought was the missing link between the formless world of spirit and the physical world of form.

I've written about Syd extensively in many of my other books, but if you haven't come across him before, he talked about the mind in terms of three spiritual principles – three fundamental elements out of which every experiential compound was created. While he called them Mind, Consciousness, and Thought, he was very clear that the words were woefully inadequate for the job of making the invisible visible.

But while words are often inadequate, they're also kind of what we've got to work with. And though they may never help us truly 'eff the ineffable,' they can act like clothes on the invisible man, allowing us to see the outline of what's really there even without being able to fully articulate what it is.

So...

You know that feeling of being alive that you sometimes get when you're fully absorbed in a favorite activity or hanging out with some of your favorite people? Your eyes spark up and start to twinkle and you're filled with good feelings and an enthusiasm for life that may seem all out of proportion to what's actually going on.

That feeling is an experience of the principle of Mind – what Syd Banks described as 'the energy and intelligence of all things, whether in form or formless.' It's the electricity we feel when we engage fully with a project or connect deeply with another living thing – the animating force that distinguishes an actual baby from a baby doll. That energy is always surrounding us and running through us, but it can be more or less obscured, depending on how caught up we are in the content of our moment-by-moment thinking.

And you know how sometimes you just know things without knowing how you know them? That's the principle of Mind in action. When something new occurs to you, it occurs via the deeper Mind. Or to put it another way, when you're in the creative flow, *what comes to mind comes from Mind.*

I sometimes talk about the principle of Mind as the intelligence behind life, in the sense that it seems to act as a sort of an organizing principle, ensuring that acorns become oak trees, planets and stars almost never bump into each other, and nearly every time you open your mouth to speak, words come out, even if you had no idea what you were going to say before you said it.

Have you ever wondered how it is that you can close your eyes and still know that the world hasn't disappeared? And how in fact sometimes when you turn your attention inward, the world feels even bigger than when you're looking out into it?

That feeling of spaciousness is the principle of Consciousness – what Syd Banks described as that which 'gives us the ability to realize the existence of life.' It's the space of meditation – the sky within which the clouds of thought create the weather of feeling and the sunshine of the deeper Mind brings everything within it to life. It's 'the blue' out of which new ideas come and never-before-thought thoughts arise.

It's the principle of Consciousness that's allowing you to read these words and make sense of them in your own mind. It's that within you that notices that which is around you – the blank page that invites you to scribble all over it and brings those scribbles to life with the skill of a Hollywood special-effects department.

What makes up those scribbles? The principle of Thought in action.

Thought – the creative force – is the most powerful scribbling pen in the universe. It lets us draw conclusions from the past and make up stories about the future. It can create heavenly experiences when our circumstances are hell, and can make us feel like hell even when everything in life seems to be going our way.

As a sort of shorthand, I sometimes share the principles in the form of three simple truths about human beings:

- We are alive (Mind).

- We are awake (Consciousness).

- We are creative (Thought).

14

The Kindness of the Design

If the three principles are the BIOS of the human operating system, the basic operating principle is this:

One hundred percent of our experience of life is created from inside the mind.

That is, contrary to the way things appear, everything we think, feel, and experience originates in the mind, not in the world. No exceptions. The system only works one way, no matter how it seems.

This is the essence of the *inside-out understanding*:

When we see that our experience only works one way – from inside to out, thought to experience, nothing to something – we recognize that our feelings and perceptions of the world will continually be changing. The nature of thought is fluid, and as we allow for that, neither dwelling on thoughts of the past nor obsessing about thoughts of the future, we spend more and more of our time living in the flow of present-moment thinking.

How clearly we see that underpins how we handle absolutely every situation in our life. For example, I have spent most of my life afraid. Not afraid of anything in particular, though at times it certainly seemed like it. I've been afraid of heights and afraid of people; afraid of spiders and afraid of snakes; afraid of failure and afraid of success. But whatever it looked like I was afraid of at any given moment, the one constant was the background sense of terror that permeated my life.

Now all that fear hasn't held me back as much as you might think. Perhaps because it was such a constant, I developed ways of dealing with it early on, from 'I think I'm going to throw up' courage to 'head in the sand' avoidance to attempting to convince myself that fear was simply 'false evidence appearing real.' As my psychological understanding grew more sophisticated, I graduated to fear-busting techniques ranging from hypnosis to autogenics and from neuro-linguistic programming (NLP) to Thought Field Therapy (TFT).

When I came across the inside-out understanding, it became apparent to me that the reason I was afraid so much of the time was because the world I was creating inside my head was such a dangerous place. So, trying to technique my way out of fear was a bit like trying to tell someone falling out of an airplane without a parachute that hitting the ground wasn't going to hurt. You might convince them of it for a moment or two while they were looking into your eyes, but as soon as they were looking down again, all bets would be off.

Over time, as I came to see that a) we live in a world of thought and b) we can always think again, my fear began to wane. I actually remember sitting on my sofa one day, thinking about the challenges of my life, and noticing that something felt different and a bit 'off.' When I tried to make sense of that unusual 'off' feeling, I realized what it was. I wasn't afraid.

While I've experienced that sense of fearlessness more and more over the ensuing years, I've still had an uncomfortable relationship with my uncomfortable feelings. So when a friend told me that she experienced fear and other 'negative emotions' as a part of the kindness of the human design, I had no idea what she was talking about.

Here (in my words) is what she said:

> Imagine the mind is like a train station. There are trains leaving all the time to any destination you can think of. Some will take you up into the mountains of ecstasy; others will take you down into the depths of despair. Some leave the station quickly, but then lose steam and drop you off in the middle of nowhere; others are slow to start but over time take you exactly where you want to go, even if you didn't know where that was when you first got on board.

> At times it's relatively easy to hop aboard the trains taking you somewhere interesting and avoid the ones taking you down a rabbit hole. But the busier the train station gets, the harder it is to navigate, and you might even find yourself hopping from train to train, feeling incredibly active and busy but never really getting anywhere in the process.

Now, imagine there was a foolproof way to instantly know whether a particular train of thought was taking you somewhere good. You wouldn't have to ride the train all the way to its destination to find out where it was headed; you could simply hop off at the next station and wait for another train to come along.

This is the role of feelings in the human system:

Whenever you feel fear, or despair, or hopelessness, or righteous anger, or any one of a host of variations on the theme, it's the design of the system letting you know where that train of thought is heading. It's not telling you anything about the world, or even about your capability – it's simply telling you there's nothing good waiting for you at the end of this particular train of thought.

The discomfort of certain feelings is there to warn you of the larger discomfort if you carry on thinking the way you're thinking. For example, you feel a little bit of pain when you accidentally put your hand too close to a flame. But that prevents you from feeling a lot of pain if you carry on toward the fire.

On the other hand, whenever you feel hope, or gratitude, or light-heartedness, or a deep sense of connection, your feelings are telling you that you're tuned into the Universal Mind with minimal interference. They're not telling you that you're *doing* the right things, but that in that moment you have clear access to your own deeper wisdom.

Perhaps the most pertinent example I could think of when I was making sense of this for myself was that of a very dear friend who had lost her brother to cot death when he was only seven months old. When her first baby boy was born many years later, he slept beside her in a clear bassinett so she could watch him while he slept. On the very first night of his life, she woke up and looked over and thought he wasn't breathing. In the midst of her panic, imagining every dark possibility, she heard a quiet voice inside her say, 'That way madness lies.' She calmed down, took another look, and saw the tiny rise and fall of her baby's chest.

For me, as a life-long scaredy cat, the idea that my 'negative emotions' are on my side has taken some getting used to. But knowing that all they are reminding me of is the fact that I'm feeling my own thinking makes them considerably less frightening.

Putting It All Together

So how does this all play out in the arena of creating in the world?

Contrary to much of what is taught as part of the empowerment model in modern psychology, we can't really choose what we think. Since we don't control which thoughts come to mind in any given moment, we can only ever 'choose' from a menu that was handed to us by our own mind. And because the energy of Thought is a constant variable, our feelings are a constant variable as well.

This turns out to be the most wonderful news in the world. Since our state of mind (thoughts and feelings) is continually changing, we don't need to put any of our energy into attempting to control it. Knowing that the natural variance of our own thinking will take us in and out of various states of mind throughout the day, we can play the game of life to the best of our abilities, regardless of how we happen to be feeling at the moment.

By way of example, imagine you've cloned one of the world's greatest golfers, so you have two physically identical versions.

Golfer One is having an amazing day. His mind is clear, he did really well on the last hole, and he's in the flow. He lines up his tee shot, takes the perfect swing, and the ball goes flying.

Golfer Two lines up exactly the same way and takes an identical swing. But he's having a terrible day. He woke up on the wrong side of the bed, blew an easy putt on the last hole, and things seem to be going from bad to worse.

Here's the question: which of the two is going to hit a better shot?

Approximately 99 out of 100 people I've asked that question of say, 'Well, the golfer who doesn't have a lot on his mind, who's clear-headed and in a good space will hit a better shot, because golf is 90 percent mental.'

But if you think you've got to feel great to play great, you'll be thinking about how you're feeling and trying to fix it or cope with the circumstances that appear, to your outside-in misunderstanding, to be involved. This hyper-focus on thoughts and feelings (as opposed to the golf ball and your target) may well interfere with your natural ability and learned skills and affect your golf shot.

If you understand that your state of mind will naturally ebb and flow and can no more cause you to perform better or worse than changes in the weather or the number of people in the gallery wearing red shirts, you can continue to play to the best of your abilities regardless.

Remember, these golfers hit identical shots. So their balls will land in exactly the same place, regardless of what they were thinking or how they were feeling when they hit them.

How does knowing this impact the creative process?

By helping us to adapt more quickly to the realities of our situation, dropping both unrealistic expectations ('This is going to be a piece of cake – we'll all be millionaires by the end of the week!') and unrealistic limitations ('This is just too damn hard – I'm too old/young/smart/dumb/experienced/inexperienced to succeed!'), so we're less likely to talk ourselves out of starting or give up before the job is done.

It also allows our common sense to guide us to follow more effective strategies and quickly abandon dead-ends and wrong turns. So we spend less time cleaning up our mess or thinking about everything that could go wrong (or right) and more time doing what needs to be done. This creates greater efficiency and opens us up to even more creative inspiration, as we experience having more than enough time to complete each successive project.

The wonderful possibility for all of us, always, is the realization of one simple yet revolutionary truth:

When we can see that our experience is only and always coming from our own mind, we no longer experience ourselves at the mercy of the world.

Some Final Thoughts...

As I mentioned in the introduction, there's a fundamental difference between understanding something intellectually and realizing it insightfully. So, while this chapter could be considered the basic course in how the human mind really works, the rest of the book will act as a series of examples, experiments, and catalysts for your own insight. And the moment you have an honest-to-goodness beyond-the-intellect insight into the inside-out nature of experience, you'll find the process of creation begins to look simpler, even if you're not quite sure what exactly it is that you've seen. Or even, perhaps, what you want to create.

In the next chapter, we'll talk more about the principle of Mind and how it functions as both the source of the creative spark and the ultimate resource for bringing your dreams to life. But before you move on, here are a few key ideas from this chapter to reflect on:

- We are alive, we are awake, and we are creative.

- One hundred percent of our experience of life is created from inside the mind.

- We live in a world of Thought, and we can always think again.

- Since our state of mind (thoughts and feelings) is continually changing, we don't need to put any of our energy into attempting to control it.

- We can always play the game of life to the best of our abilities, regardless of how we happen to be feeling at the moment.

Chapter 3

The Ultimate Resource

'The power of imagination makes us infinite.'
JOHN MUIR

Imagine you are walking along a mountain path with an invisible giant by your side. To the left of the path is a rock face extending up as far as the eye can see; to the right is a sheer drop, extending downwards into apparent nothingness.

You are excited at the prospect of finally arriving at your next destination when you see the path ahead of you is blocked by an enormous boulder.

You push with all your might, but despite your best efforts, you can only move it a few inches. Defeated but not discouraged, you decide to work smarter, not harder. You find a long and sturdy tree branch, and, using a small rock that has fallen by the side of the path, you create a lever strong enough to move the rock a full foot away from the rock wall to your left. It's a tight squeeze, but with only minimal scraping of your hands and knees, you're able to sneak through the gap and get through to the other side.

You feel an incredible sense of accomplishment at the triumphant conquering of a seemingly immovable obstacle and the near-completion of your heroic quest. Weary from your efforts but filled with the adrenaline of victory, you push on…

Now imagine you are back on the mountain path, the invisible giant once again at your side. This time, when you come across the enormous boulder, you give it a push but quickly realize your strength won't be enough to move it. You turn to the giant for assistance and it easily removes the boulder long enough for you to walk along the path and continue on your way.

You feel no particular sense of accomplishment. You don't want or need a medal for your efforts. But you do feel humbled by the enormity of the journey you have set out on and grateful for the fact that you don't have to make that journey on your own. That energy of humility and gratitude carries you effortlessly along toward your final destination...

Syd Banks described the invisible giant of the Universal Mind like this:

> *An important thing to realize is that Universal Mind and personal mind are not two minds thinking differently, but two ways of using the same mind...There is one Universal Mind, common to all, and wherever you are, it is with you, always. There is no end or limitation, nor are there boundaries, to the human mind.*

If that sounds a bit esoteric for your current mindset, think of it like an inner GPS – a factory-installed fully reliable guidance system with access to real-time data from somewhere beyond your unavoidably limited perspective. It's the pre-existing creative intelligence inside us all – the ability to think new thoughts and get insights and ideas that bring with them a renewed sense of possibility and a rush of deeper feelings.

Gaining a deeper relationship with this inner sense of knowing is the single most powerful way I know of making better decisions, producing desired results, and navigating life with more ease and grace. What it brings to the table is so far beyond the best our best thinking can muster that it's really not worth going forward without it.

Imagine you're running an art dealership and a customer arrives in search of a van Gogh for their private collection. Through your contacts, *you manage to track down a dealer in Amsterdam who promises he can get you one for only US $32 million, which will net you close to $1 million in commission and fees. Your new client agrees to leave a deposit and come back to pick up his painting in 10 days. And then you wait. And wait. And wait.*

As the days go by, you begin to panic. You start to think it won't arrive in time. What do you do?

Do you try to make your own van Gogh in case the original doesn't arrive in time? Or do you make whatever arrangements you can in case the painting is delayed, hoping for the best but preparing for the worst?

Most people in this scenario recognize there's no point in trying to fake the van Gogh. After all, no matter how good your imitation, it won't be the same as the original. Yet when faced with the choice between waiting for a creative solution to our personal or business challenges or trying to wring an answer out of our brain by worrying, it's amazing how often we choose to go with the limited thinking of our little brain over the awesome creative capacity of the Universal Mind – our innate health, wisdom, and resilience.

Cultivating Freedom of Mind

One morning I was driving my daughter Maisy to school when she asked me, 'If you had a dollar for every time you overthought things, how rich would you be?'

I laughed in recognition of the fact that in the economy of overthinkers, I would be a wealthy man indeed.

A bit later in the car ride, she noticed me staring off into space and said, 'Now you're overthinking how much you overthink things.'

Once again, she had me dead to rights.

Fortunately, I know enough not to deliberately think about how not to think so much, so after dropping her off I let my mind wander. Eventually it settled on a book I'd read many years ago, when I was first beginning to explore the relationship between personal success and our impersonal spiritual nature. It was called *The Highest Goal*, and was based on the Stanford creativity course taught by Professor Michael Ray.

Here's how he wrote about it:

> *The highest goal is simply to be in this experience of connection or truth (no matter how you refer to it) all the time. That remains a goal, of course, because this is something you spend a lifetime working toward rather than attaining. But your commitment motivates, inspires and guides your journey, and gives you more and more time in this state of connection...*
>
> *It is the experience you have when you first fall in love. Problems at work don't seem to be such problems anymore. You can handle them. You can work productively with people you may have considered enemies. You see their goodness underneath the tough exterior. You're in love. Everything looks, feels, is different.*
>
> *This kind of resonance is catalytic. Similar to a chemical catalyst, which causes reactions without being diminished, it is endlessly generative. Once you realize that it has been there for you a number of times in your life, you begin to see the enormity of it. You see that you are operating in a world in which you can draw on grace. Once you see that possibility, you can begin to act with intention relative to the highest goal and better align your efforts with this generative process.*

At first, people tend to experience that invisible spiritual energy bubbling up inside them as a resource – a spark that brings creative ideas to life. They 'awaken the giant within' and practice living their lives with 'unlimited power.' But over time, they recognize the energy as the source and themselves as the ultimate resource – a vehicle 'to be used,' in the words of the playwright George Bernard Shaw, 'for a purpose recognized by ourselves as a mighty one.'

This is my own highest goal: to live in and from my connection with the highest and best I have inside me, basking in the glow of spirit and acting as a beacon of light in the world.

And in all honesty, I'm terrible at it. As Maisy knows, I overthink pretty much everything. I try too hard. I get discouraged and downhearted. But then I find my feet again. Something new comes to mind and I remember that something new *always* comes to mind – it's built into the system. I feel hope. I have fun. I move forward. I create.

And as soon as I forget that I'm supposed to be creative, I remember how much I love to get out of the way, open up to the creative flow, and find out what happens next.

This state of flow, or 'freedom of mind,' is how we're designed to operate. It carries with it a sense of ease and clarity that brings out our common sense and leads to higher levels of performance in whatever we do. We become less distracted by our own thinking and more receptive to a deeper wisdom that comes through from somewhere beyond our brain's collection of memories and personal thinking.

We're less inclined to live in our head and more inclined to live in the moment. And because we're spending more time living in the moment without too much on our mind, we see more clearly and connect more deeply with those around us. Life becomes more of a game to be played than a gauntlet to be survived, and we spend more and more time in the experience of creative flow.

Putting It All Together

To better understand how this works, imagine a pipe that is open at both ends. Water flows easily through it, and the bigger the pipe, the more water can flow through it.

Now imagine that the outflow of the pipe gets blocked. Water still comes in, but as it has nowhere to go, it begins to back up, and the pipe gets filled up and the flow gets backed up. Eventually, if the outflow stays blocked, either the pipe will lose its integrity and start springing leaks or the water will find another path out into the world.

Or imagine that the outflow is open but the intake is blocked. Depending on the size of the pipe, water will continue to flow out for a while, but after a time it will dry up.

This is what happens when we experience a creative block. In the first scenario, we keep inputting information and ideas from anywhere we can find them, but never actually get around to creating anything in the world. Eventually, we get so overloaded that we feel that our head is going to explode and we shut down.

In the second scenario, we get cut off from the inspiration of the creative force and are forced to try and create from what we already know, which is a limited and ultimately non-renewable resource.

Here's another way of looking at it:

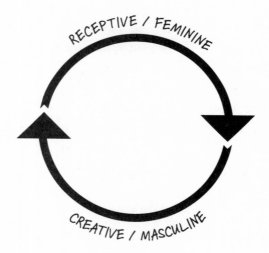

There is a continual flow from the receptive to the creative and back again. It's the dance between the feminine and the masculine, yin and yang, not doing and doing.

When we get stuck, it's either because we've stopped listening to life and closed ourselves off from the creative force or because we've stopped acting on our creative inclinations. When we get out of the way and see what happens, the creative force inevitably comes through.

And over time, if we let it, that same creative force will expand and shape us into an ever more perfect conduit for creation.

Some Final Thoughts...

In the next chapter we'll be exploring how to increase our productivity without working harder or adding any additional pressure or stress into the system.

But first, here are a few key ideas from this chapter for you to reflect on:

- 'There is no end or limitation, nor are there boundaries, to the human mind.' (Syd Banks)

- Cultivating a deeper relationship with your inner sense of knowing is the single most powerful way to begin making better decisions, producing desired results, and navigating life with more ease and grace.

- The 'highest goal' is to live in and from our connection to the highest and best we have inside us.

- Get out of the way, open up to the creative flow, and see what happens.

Chapter 4
The Secrets of Effortless Productivity

'It is necessary to be slightly underemployed
if you are to do something significant.'
JAMES B. WATSON

Candace Pert was the neuroscientist whose research led to the discovery of opiate receptors. She was a true pioneer in the field of mind–body medicine. I was fortunate to meet and work with her for a short period before her untimely death.

My first meeting with Candace came in Carlsbad, California, in 2006, at Louise Hay's 80th birthday party. My memory of her is indelibly linked with the scene from *The Matrix* where Neo is distracted by the girl in the red dress – a sudden vision of vital energy in a bold red dress being introduced to me in a whirlwind, then taking my arm and walking me around the party, asking me about my work and sharing her research into an HIV vaccine in the casual way you might expect somebody to tell you about their dry-cleaning business.

I remembered that meeting a year or so later when I was looking for someone to write the foreword to my second book, *Feel Happy Now!*, one of my early attempts at unraveling the mysteries of depression and anxiety and giving people tools for a happier life. I knew what I was sharing genuinely helped people to feel better; I was hoping Candace would be able to explain a little bit about why that was so.

She remembered me, but apologetically explained that she was far too busy trying to deal with fundraising and government red tape around her AIDS and HIV research, and while she was sure it was a wonderful book, she just didn't have time to read it.

Something about her vibrantly chaotic energy made me smile, and I was as surprised as she was to hear what came out of my mouth next: 'I'll work for you as your personal assistant for as long as it takes you to read my book if you'll consider writing the foreword if you like it.'

She was understandably reluctant – I was a self-help author she'd met one time who was living on the other side of the country – but I made her an offer she couldn't refuse: 'Give me the task you're dreading most and I'll take care of it in exchange for you considering my offer.'

A few minutes later, I was on the phone to a government official in Washington, DC, explaining that Dr Pert was no longer going to be working with his department and no, she wasn't available to talk with him, and no, this was not negotiable. When I phoned her back an hour later to let her know it was done, she reluctantly relented and told me to send her my manuscript.

Over the next six weeks, she told me she loved the book and then agreed and 'un-agreed' to write the foreword three separate times, swayed one way by her appreciation for the book and the other way by her workload.

When I told her I only had a week left before the final edit had to be with the publisher, she agreed for a fourth time. But in retrospect I shouldn't have been surprised when with three days to go she emailed me to drop out for apparently the final time.

What it was that possessed me to reach out to her from a space of playful creativity instead of frustration or anger, I don't know, but after making a quick call to Hawaii, I phoned her back with my final offer.

'Candace,' I said, 'I'll get you a personally signed photograph of Josh Holloway with his shirt open if you'll write the foreword and get it to me in the next 72 hours.'

For some reason I remembered her expressing glowing admiration for the visual impact of the actor (who played Sawyer in the TV series *Lost*) when we first met, and somehow that offer did the trick. She sent me the foreword the next morning, the book made it to the publisher in time, and Josh very kindly delivered a glossy photograph with a personal message to Candace written across his clean shaven, gently oiled chest.

I only saw Candace one more time after that, about a year later, at a conference. She walked straight over to me, glowing with life, and wrapped me in a bear hug that almost lifted me off the ground.

'That picture you sent me is sitting in a frame on my mantelpiece. My husband doesn't really like it,' she said slyly, 'but I love it!'

She then let out a big belly laugh and made her way out of the room. And that's how I'll always remember her – the woman who discovered opiate receptors, naturally high on the brain chemistry she'd decoded, full of life and love and joy.

I often think of that story when I'm explaining the secrets of effortless productivity, because it so clearly points to the non-linear and at times seemingly random nature of how things get created in the real world. While we like to make creating results mathematical and predictable in order to better plan for the future, when it comes to creating the big stuff, things tend to happen in highly unpredictable and even remarkable ways.

Beyond Busyness

A couple of years ago I was chatting with the *über*-author Jack Canfield and I asked him if he was busy at the moment. He took a few seconds to consider his reply. 'I've got a lot on,' he said, 'but I'm not particularly busy.'

This points to a key distinction made in Cal Newport's insightful book *Deep Work*: busyness is often a substitute for productivity, not its cause.

According to Professor Newport, one of the reasons we spend so much time on email, social media, and 'available' to interruption is because it creates the experience of being continually engaged in activity, which leads us to the false conclusion that if we're busy, we're being productive. Yet a more practical definition of productivity is this:

The ratio between your effort and the reward you get for that effort.

Notice this has nothing to do with our level of activity, busyness, hard work, or stress. If we get high levels of reward for each effort, we are highly productive; if we don't, no matter how much time and energy we're putting into the job, we aren't. As Sun Tzu says in *The Art of War*, 'What is essential in war is victory, not prolonged operations.'

Yet typical productivity systems are based on the idea that there is always a 1:1 ratio between effort and reward, so essentially one unit of effort will bring one unit of reward. If you want to increase the amount of reward, you need to increase the amount of effort. That's why time and productivity management systems abound. In the 1:1 model, productivity is a numbers game where you always need to *do* more to *get* more.

Contrast that with a time when you experienced diminishing returns. Perhaps you were exhausted, or you'd been working on something for so long you couldn't see the wood for the trees. In those situations, we could say the ratio of effort to reward was 3:1, where it took at least three units of effort to receive that same one unit of reward.

Or let's turn that experience on its head. What if it were possible to experience exponential returns on your efforts? So that instead of 3:1 or even 1:1, you experienced 1:2, 1:3, 1:5, all the way up to 1: infinity. I call this high reward to effort ratio 'effortless productivity,' not because you don't do anything, but rather because your rewards for your efforts are way out of proportion to the amount of effort you actually put in.

Here's another way to think about it:

Higher levels of productivity don't come from finding ways to squeeze more oranges; they come from getting more juice to the squeeze.

This doesn't mean that you don't have to put in the hours. I don't know anyone who consistently produces quality results over time who doesn't. But whether those hours are experienced as hard work or even busyness is nothing more than a reflection of your state of mind. And how much you get out of those hours is a function of two simple variables...

1. Are you having fun yet?

My friend and mentor Dr George Pransky has spent a fair bit of time exploring this kind of effortless productivity – what it is that causes us to get more (or less) bang for our buck out of everything we do. One of his observations has been that people are generally at their most productive in the parts of their work that they enjoy and least productive in the parts that they dislike, resent, or even hate.

In fact, as explained by Marcus Buckingham in his book *The One Thing You Need to Know*, a Gallup study into people who had been at or near the top of their field for a minimum of 20 years showed that the one thing they all had in common was that they had figured out what they didn't like doing and stopped doing it.

While this may seem like common sense, when you can't afford (or don't want) to get someone else to do the bits of your work you don't like doing, you probably do what most people do – procrastinate for as long as you possibly can, and then, when you really have to do them, get them over with in the quickest and least painful way you can think of. Although 'getting it over with' is certainly more productive than 'never getting round to it in the first place,' it's not an efficient long-term strategy. And things done in a white-knuckle 'just gotta get through it' frame of mind rarely go as well as they otherwise might.

So what's the alternative?

Simple. Begin to enjoy *everything* you do.

Now at first glance this seems to be a patently ridiculous and possibly even impossible challenge. After all, how do I make myself enjoy catching up on a backlog of email, making cold calls, asking the bank for money, or whatever part of my work I think of as a 'necessary evil'?

But the thing is, our preferences aren't written in stone. In fact, most of them are the somewhat arbitrary consequence of childhood incidents, cultural conditioning, and psychological reinforcement. So much of what we enjoy or don't enjoy is based on limited or even second-hand experience, perpetuated unwittingly by the thought *I don't like that.*

For example, as a girl, my wife was forced to drink warm milk that had been sitting in the sun in the schoolyard and it made her physically ill. That experience was passed on to our kids, who grew up hating milk without ever really having tried it. But in my house, we grew up enjoying milk on our breakfast cereal, milk with our after-school snacks, and a glass of milk with our dinner. And my sister's adult children still drink milk every day.

All of us have the wonderful possibility of dropping our acquired preferences and returning to our natural mode of indiscriminate enjoyment at any moment. Each time we get past our thinking and into whatever it is that we're doing, we learn more and do better. Over time, that indiscriminate enjoyment leads to higher levels of engagement and a natural boost in our levels of seemingly effortless productivity.

(As a brief postscript, in the middle of writing this, I stepped outside to discover that my dog had left a huge pile of poo outside my office door. After a brief flurry of thoughts about the relative merits of pet ownership and what a pain it was to have to clean up after a dog when I was trying to write important things about people, I laughed at myself and decided to see what it was like to enjoy cleaning up dog poo. Less than five minutes later, the whole area was cleaned up, hosed down, and looking better than it had in weeks. And I thanked my dog for the clearly carefully planned reminder...)

2. Are you all in?

One of my all-time favorite quotes about the second 'secret' to effortless productivity comes from the playwright George Bernard Shaw, who wrote:

> *This is the true joy in life, the being used for a purpose recognized by yourself as a mighty one; the being thoroughly worn out before you are thrown on the scrap heap; the being a force of Nature instead of a feverish selfish little clod of ailments and grievances complaining that the world will not devote itself to making you happy.*

One of the things that makes us better at whatever it is we do is to participate fully, express ourselves fully, and give ourselves over to whatever it is we're doing. Or to put it another way, to get more out of anything we do, we first need to put more of ourselves into it.

As with enjoyment, indiscriminate full engagement is our natural state. Think of a baby staring at a mobile, playing peek-a-boo with a parent, or discovering the joy of having hands and feet. They are undistracted by extraneous mental activity and fully engaged in the task at hand. By way of contrast, look around at adults as they sleepwalk through life, preoccupied with their problems, distracted by their devices, and, in the words of Neil Postman, 'amusing themselves to death.'

As long as we're debating whether or not we should be doing what we're doing, more than half of our energy is lost in that internal conversation. We get so caught up with questioning what we're doing that there's no space left in our head for fresh ideas about how to do it. It's like driving a car with a 12-cylinder engine but only two cylinders firing – everything feels like an uphill climb.

Once we go all in and throw ourselves into whatever we're doing, all of that mental chatter fades away and we're free to be inspired about and creative with what's in front of us. Full engagement is a game-changer, because everything starts to feel easier. Like driving that same car with the big engine firing on all cylinders, once we throw ourselves into any endeavor, even the steepest challenge feels well within our capacity.

Putting It All Together

The beauty of this approach to productivity is that it feeds on itself:

- When I'm enjoying myself, I have a much richer experience of whatever it is that I'm doing. I'm less distracted, more present, and able to ride the stresses, strains, and variances of a typical day with a lot more ease and grace.

- When I'm fully engaged, I perform better. I'm able to contribute more. I'm incredibly capable. I'm surprisingly wise. My curiosity is unleashed, everything becomes fascinating, and I inevitably begin to enjoy whatever it is that I'm doing.

In short:

Enjoyment leads to engagement; engagement leads to enjoyment. And engagement and enjoyment lead to more bang for your buck, more juice to the squeeze, and a higher ratio of reward for every effort.

Or as Henry David Thoreau once said, 'If one advances confidently in the direction of his dreams and endeavors to live the life which he has imagined, he will meet with a success unexpected in common hours.'

In this sense, effortless productivity isn't about working harder, or even smarter. It's about showing up to a project with a sense of play and a heart full of joy, fully committed to the task at hand and completely open to whatever may come. It's about throwing yourself into things as if your life depended on it while knowing full well that it doesn't.

Whenever you do this, your connection to the invisible giant of the Universal Mind grows stronger. I can't tell you exactly how this works, but I can tell you that it always happens. Because while ideas and opportunities rarely unfold the way we think they're going to, they do unfold. Each time we go to the 'Big Nothing' of the creative unknown, new ideas and opportunities will come. And knowing that is worth its weight in gold.

Some Final Thoughts...

Here are a few things to reflect on before you move forward:

- When it comes to creating the impossible, our levels of productivity and effectiveness are inherently non-linear.

- Productivity is a measure of the ratio between effort and reward. To become more productive, we need to improve that ratio so that we're getting more reward for each effort. To put it another way, increased productivity doesn't come from finding new ways to squeeze more oranges; it comes from getting more juice to the squeeze.

- Indiscriminate enjoyment and engagement are completely natural and the keys to effortless productivity.

- When you throw yourself into whatever you are doing as if your life depended on it, knowing full well that it doesn't, you will 'meet with a success unexpected in common hours.'

~

Chapter 5

Creating the Future
for Fun and Profit

'The future cannot be predicted, but futures can be invented.'
Dennis Gabor

I once worked with a man who over the years had built up several successful bars and restaurants. His current endeavor, however, was struggling, mired in a swamp of temperamental staff, rising rents, and a 'custody battle' with his business partner and investors over which of them had the right to set the direction for the future.

During one of our sessions, he shared that his partner had offered him the opportunity to back out of the project entirely, with minimal debt, if he left immediately. His hesitation was because he felt that without his continued presence, the project was doomed to failure, and he owed it to the investors not to let it go down without a fight.

'I've only got two choices,' he said to me. 'Save myself and leave my investors to drown, or fight like hell to right the ship, even though everyone on board, including the investors, wants me to leave.'

When I pressed him on why those were his only two choices, the source of his apparent dilemma became clear. 'There's no way that place will survive without me,' he said.

Now understand, that statement wasn't as arrogant as it might first sound. His presence and personality were two of the main reasons why people patronized the business in the first place. But what he couldn't see was that the reason he felt between a rock and a hard place was because he was unwilling to question his imaginary future. As long as he believed 'the business can't survive without me,' any course of action that would take him away from the business was the equivalent of abandoning a sinking ship with the women and children still on board.

I explained to him that the mind works like a virtual reality generator – whatever we think about seems real to us for as long as we're thinking it; the more we think about it, the more real it seems. So the fact that he couldn't imagine a scenario where the business survived without him was simply evidence for how the mind works, not an accurate prediction of the future.

The other reason we can't accurately predict the future is that there's no way to predict what will occur to us and for us as we move forward. In this case, while the business was currently set up around my client being a part of it, if he were no longer there, a whole new approach to customer satisfaction might occur to his partner, one not predicated on his presence. In fact, the business's over-reliance on his force of personality might well have been masking a host of problems and opportunities that would become evident in the vacuum left by his departure.

I went on to share one of my favorite stories from *The Cherry Log Sermons* by the Reverend Fred Craddock, who was apparently visiting family when he struck up an unlikely conversation with an old greyhound his niece had recently adopted:

> *I said to the dog, 'Are you still racing?'*
>
> *'No,' the dog replied.*
>
> *'Well, what was the matter? Did you get too old to race?'*
>
> *'No, I still had some race in me.'*
>
> *'Well, what then? Did you not win?'*
>
> *'I won over a million dollars for my owner.'*
>
> *'Well, what was it? Bad treatment?'*

'Oh, no,' the dog said. 'They treated us royally when we were racing.'

'Did you get crippled?'

'No.'

'Then why?' I pressed. 'Why?'

The dog answered, 'I quit.'

'You quit?'

'Yes,' he said. 'I quit.'

'Why did you quit?'

'I just quit because after all that running and running and running, I found out that the rabbit I was chasing wasn't even real.'

The future is like this too. Not only is it unpredictable, but there's actually no such thing as 'the future' to begin with. The whole idea is made up in our own mind.

Sometimes our thoughts make up a possible future that we like and we dwell on it; other times they make one up that freaks us out and we do our best to move on. But our scary thoughts about the future don't predict failure any more than our positive thoughts about the future guarantee success. What they do do is distract us from the rich inner resources we have to respond to what's happening now.

While the idea that my client's business might do as well or better without him there was clearly difficult for him to hear, it opened up the possibility of an infinite number of futures where he was neither the villain nor the hero of the day. And that in turn opened up the space for him to explore what he actually wanted to do, regardless of which way things ultimately turned out for the business.

What I've seen over the years is that when you lose your taste for predicting the future, you develop a palate for the offerings of the present moment. You discover that previously undreamed-of possibilities and unimagined opportunities present themselves with astonishing regularity. And whatever temporary peace of mind you give up in letting go of the illusion that you can accurately predict the future, you gain back in the knowledge that you can consistently create it.

How do you do that?

The Ultimate Formula for Successful Creation

There are only two steps to creating anything you want in the world:

1. Show up and begin moving in the direction of your dreams.

2. Respond to what shows up along the way.

Before you dismiss the strategy out of hand in search of something more complicated, let's see if I can complicate it enough for you to give it a try...

In the late 1990s, our cat, Mason, was hit by a car outside our house in London the day after we moved in. While we missed him terribly, it woke us up to the fact that the corner we lived on was a busy one, and children and animals were continually risking life and limb to run across the intersection to the park across the street.

While I had no idea how to even begin the process of getting a pedestrian crossing (known as a 'zebra crossing' in the UK) put in, I knew that if I showed up to the problem and took the first step, at some point the next step would appear.

An internet search showed me that our local MP (Member of Parliament) would be the first port of call; a phone call revealed that she held a weekly 'surgery' not far from our house, where members of her constituency could stand in line to request her assistance with their community-based concerns.

During our meeting, I found out that we needed a minimum of 1,000 signatures to get a feasibility study for the crosswalk commissioned. I didn't know how to go about getting them, but I figured if I showed up, something would happen, so I went and stood by the park with a stack of lined paper and a clipboard. After about an hour, someone appeared who had begun a similar petition; we agreed to share resources over a coffee in the park. The woman who owned the café we were in overheard our conversation and offered to 'host' the petition by her cash register, and less than a month after showing up to the project I presented our MP with the 1,000 signatures.

The entire process took just over two years and we had left the country by the time the crosswalk was complete, but I was delighted to visit it on a subsequent visit back to London and surreptitiously christen it the inadvertently cross-species 'Mason the Cat Zebra Crossing.'

At no point did I know how or even if the project would be successful. What I did know was that whenever we show up and aim ourselves in a direction, the impersonal creative intelligence behind life shows up with us.

If we let it, the force that grows islands out of underwater volcanos and brings babies out of women's tummies puts ideas in our head, words in our mouth, and opportunities in our path. It's not magic – it's just how it works.

Here's another example. One day I was running a mastermind group and I asked each of the participants to prepare and deliver a 90-second audition for a TED Talk, sharing their 'idea worth spreading.' While the topics varied from Google's Andromeda project to experiencing God on a visit to death row, the purpose of the exercise was the same in every case: to heighten the participants' awareness of the fact that we invariably experience a wide range of thinking when we begin heading in a new direction.

By their own reports, in the moments before each of them got up to speak that thinking ranged from *Oh my God, why does he want us to do this?* to *It's so unfair – I haven't had enough time to prepare* to *I think I'm going to be sick* to my personal favorite, *F#%k off, Michael Neill*, a sentiment that apparently comes up often enough for the group to have abbreviated it to the simple acronym FOMN.

Yet somewhere in that swirl of thinking, a deeper part of the mind guided every one of those people to dismiss the noise of that thinking and step out onto the stage anyway. When they did, new thoughts occurred, ranging from *I'd better just get this over with* to *I'm among friends – this is going to be fun* to *I'm looking forward to sharing this* to *I wonder where I'm going to begin?*

The background noise of their personal thinking carried on for most of the group throughout their auditions, yet at no point did it seem sufficiently compelling to stop them from moving forward or knock them off-track once they'd begun.

In other words, when it comes to creating what we want to see in the world, 'positive thinking' is no more of a boost than 'negative thinking' is an obstacle – it's all just noise in a system that's both designed to handle noise and to give us exactly what we need exactly when we need it.

My own TEDx talk, 'Why Aren't We Awesomer?', began life as a very different idea. I initially thought it might be fun to organize a TEDx event in Los Angeles. That possibility led to my sending one of my apprentices, Barbara Patterson, to a planning meeting, which in turn led to her doing a TEDx talk called 'I Don't Have a Plan and I've Never Been More On Purpose.'

While hosting an event quickly became unfeasible, the idea of doing a talk of my own came in to take its place. About six months later, one of my students from my coach training school, Supercoach Academy, reached out to ask if I'd be interested in being a speaker at TEDx Bend, one of the largest annual TEDx events in America. She admitted, however, that they already had a speaker lined up who might be a bit too similar to me, so I'd have to have an interview with the head of the selection committee and the odds were stacked against me.

My son was going to university about two hours away from Bend and I thought the whole thing could be fun and a good father–son bonding experience, so I agreed to the interview.

When the head of the selection committee called me on my cell phone, I was sitting outside my daughter's dance studio waiting to pick her up from class. He began by telling me why they probably wouldn't choose me (which actually put me at my ease) and then asked me: 'So, what's your idea worth spreading?'

While in retrospect this was a somewhat obvious question, I hadn't prepared an answer. I knew enough about the responsive nature of the mind not to panic, so I gave myself time to pause and to show up fully to the question. And then, after a few moments, I began to speak.

'Well, the mind works more like a projector than a camera...'

Before I could get a second sentence out, he interrupted to tell me that he was extremely interested and would be recommending me to the committee.

A few weeks later I got my formal invitation, and the rest, at least in my little corner of the world, is history.

The point of all this storytelling is simply this – if you take a fresh look at it, you'll see that a remarkable amount of success in the world comes down to people staying in the game long enough to get lucky. Fortunately, 'luck' is a predictable part of the process.

In other words, you can rest assured that when you show up to your life and start moving in a direction, the creative potential of the deeper Mind will show up with you. And you can have equal faith in the fact that if you keep moving in the direction of your goals and dreams, fresh possibilities and previously unseen opportunities will begin to emerge.

Here's a simple rule of thumb:

As you begin moving in the direction of your dreams, the emergence of fresh new thinking and unexpected synchronicities (i.e. 'luck') is 100 percent reliable and 98 percent unpredictable.

Putting It All Together

One of the questions that people often ask is: 'If creating is so straight-forward, why do we so often struggle to create "the big stuff" in our lives?'

In my experience, there are actually a number of very good reasons for that...

Most of us are terrible at making decisions and committing to them

This is because we try to use the weakest part of ourselves to do it – our personal willpower. Since most of us haven't developed our willpower in that way, we give up early in the game and use that fact to beat ourselves up and talk ourselves out of even starting next time.

But what we can do and are generally really good at is following the flow of our common sense and wisdom. And when we see that we have a sense of direction – an inner GPS – and know it's always on, it helps us to navigate the not yet created world of pure possibility and creative potential.

We don't really understand the creative process

We tend to think of creativity as a series of steps we have to take rather than a naturally unfolding process we can make use of. It's like the difference between walking and trying to tell someone how to walk. We walk by making use of thousands of complex muscle movements that are well suited to our biological mechanism, honed by tens of thousands of hours of trial and learning. We can break down the 'steps,' but, as Mark Twain said, 'If people learned to walk and talk the way we teach them to read and write, everybody would limp and stutter.'

We totally misunderstand the feeling of being stuck

We think it's like being stuck in traffic, or in the mud – being caught up in something outside ourselves that's genuinely fixed and immovable. But we're not really stuck in that sense – we're stuck in our *head*. We can't see a way forward, and that often sets off a ton of habitual thinking about why we're stuck, what our psychological blocks are, and how long it's going to take us to get past them all.

The good news is that the only thing that ever gets truly stuck is our own thinking. And we're never more than one thought away from being back in our own creative flow.

We forget that as a general rule, it takes time to create stuff in the world

The comedian Louis C.K. once joked that if you set out on a cross-country journey in the 1800s, with all the births and deaths and people dropping out along the way, a whole different group of people would arrive at the end.

In the same way, as we set out on our own journey to creating the impossible, our thoughts begin to change and the world starts to look different. When we keep showing up and keep acting and responding, new things get created and the world starts to *be* different.

Some Final Thoughts...

Perhaps the most important thing to remember about creating is simply this:

Now is the moment of creation.

We can only wield the magic paintbrush of thought on the blank canvas of consciousness at this very moment. After enough moments, a picture begins to emerge from a series of seemingly disconnected brushstrokes. And as what at first existed only in our imagination begins to come into form, other people begin to see it as well and become enrolled in the possibility of its creation.

We're already designed for success in any creative endeavor – it's just that we've learned to make things far more complicated than they need to be and our ego and intellect far more important to the creative process than they actually are. Each time we simply show up and respond to what shows up without a personal agenda, a need to prove anything, or a lot of thinking about how this task will fit into the grand picture of our life, the creative force shows up with us.

As we bring the first part of this book to a close, I want to invite you to let it settle in without trying too hard to remember any of the key ideas or practice anything as a 'technique.'

In fact, there's no need to turn *any* of these ideas into new methodologies to be practiced in any kind of a systematic way. Whatever you've seen for yourself so far is already yours; you'll know that you really see it because it will organically change the way you approach creating what you want in the world. What you don't yet see will remain up for grabs, and the chance of seeing something new is permanently available. As my mentor Mavis Karn once pointed out, 'We will never know this little again,' so we can be grateful for what we've got and hopeful about what is yet to come.

In the next part of the book, you'll get the chance to put your insights into action as you actively create an impossible project in your own life. Even if you decide not to do the program over the course of 90 days, you'll find that the bite-sized reminders and multiple examples will act as catalysts to help you see these truths more clearly and bring your impossible dreams to life with less stress, more ease, and an expanded sense of what's possible.

But first, here are a few key points to consider from this chapter...

- 'The future cannot be predicted, but futures can be invented.' (Dennis Gabor)

- The mind works like a virtual reality generator – whatever we think about seems real to us for as long as we're thinking it; the more we think about it, the more real it seems.

- The ultimate formula for successful creation is to show up, begin moving in a direction, and respond to what shows up along the way.

- Whatever it is that you're up to, the emergence of fresh new thinking and unexpected synchronicities (i.e. 'luck') is 100 percent reliable and 98 percent unpredictable.

- Now is the moment of creation.

~

PART II

MAKING THE IMPOSSIBLE POSSIBLE

'It's kind of fun to do the impossible.'

Where the Rubber Meets the Road

'Reality is wrong. Dreams are for real.'
TUPAC SHAKUR

Welcome to Part II of *Creating the Impossible*!

In this section of the book I'll be guiding you through a 90-day program to bring an impossible dream to life. The program picks up on all of the themes we've been exploring so far and breaks them down into bite-sized chunks that you can use as a structure to support you along the way. But because the process of creation is inherently non-linear, you don't have to follow the steps in order.

Here are a few different ways you can use the program:

- *As designed* – go through the lessons in order, day by day, for the next 13 weeks.

Each week begins with an 'impossible challenge' – an exercise that will help you get a feel for how the principles behind creation play out in the everyday experience of our lives. You can do one or all of the impossible challenges separately from the rest of the program. You'll find the resulting insights will impact the way you show up in your work, even before you have a seemingly impossible project to work on.

Each day contains a quote and a brief essay designed to serve as a catalyst for your own insight and inspiration. Some of the days also include a suggestion for an exercise or experiment, and every seventh day I encourage you to take the day off to rest, review, recharge, and renew your commitment to your impossible project.

- *As a 'coach on demand'* for support in creating your impossible dream in your own way. Want to create some momentum? Go to Week 5. Feeling stuck? Go to Week 9.

- *As a kind of 'oracle.'* Simply open this part of the book to a random page and see what that day has in store for you!

However you choose to use the program, I recommend you also take advantage of the seven-day online video jumpstart to give yourself a boost at the beginning of any new endeavor. You'll find the link and exclusive access code in the appendix at the end of the book.

'What if I Don't Know What I Want to Create?'

One of the most frustrating obstacles for people who participate in our online program is when they feel that they're supposed to know what their impossible project is before they begin.

While you may already know exactly what you want to create, many of us are so used to only going after what we think is 'realistic' – generally speaking, whatever we've accomplished in the past plus up to 50 percent more – that when we start looking for something that seems impossible we don't even know where to begin. The trick is that you don't have to know before you start. The moment you declare yourself 'in the game,' you'll come to realize that the game has already begun!

Here are a couple of guidelines for choosing your impossible project:

1. Choose something you don't really believe can happen, but would love if it did

I recounted one of my favorite examples of this in *You Can Have What You Want*:

Rebecca, a client of mine from London, was visiting Los Angeles. She was beautiful, intelligent, and strong, but she'd spent most of her life pretending she wasn't so she wouldn't upset anyone.

During one of our sessions, I shared with her what I consider to be one of the golden rules of creation: 'It's easier to create what you really want than what you think you can get.'

Her response was to laugh in my face. 'If that were true,' she said, 'I'd be going out with a sexy movie star this evening instead of back to my hotel room alone.'

Although she was joking, I could feel the energy in the room lighten up as she confessed to an authentic if unlikely desire.

Here's what happened...

When she got back to her hotel, she decided to lie out by the pool. Suddenly, she overheard two people talking excitedly on some nearby sun-loungers. 'Isn't that...? Oh my God, I think it is!'

She looked up and sure enough, a sexy (in her humble opinion) movie star was walking toward the pool, looking for somewhere to sit. And there just happened to be an available lounger right next to her.

While I have no idea what happened next, she phoned me the next day sounding as though she was awakening from a wonderful dream.

'It really happened!' she said excitedly. 'Just imagine what it would be like if I let myself do this with the rest of my life!'

Notice that Rebecca didn't believe it was possible, and she certainly didn't believe in herself. She just thought it sounded like a game worth playing, regardless of what actually did happen. She created the game through expressing an authentic desire that had previously seemed too silly/unlikely/impossible to even consider. And something shifted inside her that made the 'impossible' possible.

2. Know that you will probably lose – and play to win!

When I first began working with a life coach many years ago, he challenged me to create an impossible game around money. With his coaching support, I set up a 90-day game where 'winning' was defined as earning more than I had earned in the previous 12 months.

What was interesting to me was just how hard it was for me to even write my 'impossible' goal down, let alone say it out loud. It was as if setting a goal and failing to achieve it was the worst thing that could possibly happen to me.

Each time I pointed out to my coach that I didn't think I could possibly win my self-proclaimed money game, he would just say, 'That's okay – if you couldn't lose, it wouldn't be much of a game.'

I found that thought oddly comforting, but it wasn't until I read *The Last Word on Power* by Tracy Goss that I began to understand why.

Here's how she puts it:

> *Leadership always includes knowledge of the possibility*
> *of failure. In [an impossible] game, that produces a*
> *remarkable degree of confidence. If you operate with*
> *an acceptance of failure, you will remain confident no*
> *matter what happens during the course of the game.*

> *You still play 'to win,' of course, as without that, there would be*
> *no game at all. And there is always a scoreboard – you kept your*
> *bold promise [achieved your goal] or you didn't. You check the*
> *scoreboard when the whistle blows ... but the game never ends.*

> *You calculate the results and debrief on how you 'played.'*
> *What's important, because you said so, is that you move the*
> *possibility forward. That allows you to immerse yourself*
> *in the challenge and pleasure of your game, regardless*
> *of the impediments you encounter or the circumstances*
> *that you must include. They are all opportunities for*
> *building the muscles of making the impossible happen.*

As it happens, I failed at the money game – I didn't reach my target until halfway through the fourth month. But along the way I realized that the more I helped my clients to achieve their impossible dreams, the more my own impossible dreams began to come true.

While I don't always look to comedians for my inspiration, this thought from Jim Carrey is worth contemplating:

'You can fail at what you don't want, so you might as well take a chance on doing what you love.'

Let the games begin!

With all my love,

Michael

WEEK 1

CHOOSING YOUR IMPOSSIBLE PROJECT

'You don't have to be a fantastic hero to do certain things – to compete. You can be just an ordinary chap, sufficiently motivated to reach challenging goals.'

SIR EDMUND HILLARY

This week, we'll begin the process of choosing an impossible project for you to work with over the course of this program. Even if you're already pretty sure about what you want to create, go through each day in turn. Worst case, you'll find it fun to daydream about cool stuff showing up in your life. Best case, something will be prompted in you that becomes the kernel or core of your impossible project.

Having guided thousands of people through this process, the best advice I can give you is to watch out for 'premature practicality.' What sometimes makes it difficult to choose an impossible project is that we're so conditioned to only attempt what we think we can succeed at that we take a whole bunch of things off the menu before we even begin.

If you want a quick rule of thumb for choosing a great project, ask yourself:

Does the thought of it make me gasp, grin, or giggle?

IMPOSSIBLE CHALLENGE NO.1: TAKE FIVE

Each day this week, 'take five' at least once:

- Sit for five minutes.
- Don't get up.
- Don't talk, write, or engage in any other obvious external distractions.
- Let your mind go wherever it wants.

There's no way to get this wrong — as long as you remain sitting (you can move about in your seat if you like), you're meeting the challenge.

DAY 1

Pipe Dreams and Possibilities

'The future belongs to those who believe
in the beauty of their dreams.'

ELEANOR ROOSEVELT

I've noticed that there are certain things it's fun to think about. I like fantasizing about world leaders reading my books, seeing the innocent error of their outside-in thinking, and turning their lives and policies around to bring them more into line with their innate wisdom. I think it would be cool to stand atop Mt Everest, sip tea with the Dalai Lama, and play a game of flag football with Tom Brady.

This kind of 'pipe dreaming' doesn't seem to diminish my appreciation of the present moment and over the years has attuned my mind to possibilities that I might otherwise have missed. When the opportunity to step into one of my pipe dreams and make it real arises, I sometimes do. This doesn't mean that the dream becomes a goal; it skips that step and goes straight from pipe dream to possibility to project.

Once something has become a project, I'm either working on it or I'm not. When I am, it's a part of my 'now'; when I'm not, it's not. This frees me up to stay creatively engaged with the present moment, regardless of what it contains or whether or not it will ultimately 'get me' anywhere.

I've noticed that when I'm creatively engaged, I tend to do good work. Good work often leads to good results, and good results often lead to more opportunities in the world.

So here's a question for you:

What would you love to create in your life, in your work, or in the world, even if you knew you would probably fail?

And here's an experiment to help you answer that question:

Finish the following sentence as many times as you can throughout the day:

● Wouldn't it be cool if...?

Examples:

● Wouldn't it be cool if I invented a new kind of coffee that would automatically adjust its caffeine levels to my body's needs?

● Wouldn't it be cool if my bank balance had two extra zeros on it?

● Wouldn't it be cool if I could teleport so that I didn't have to sit in traffic and could just literally go from one place to another without a gap?

● Wouldn't it be cool if that person I've been admiring from afar was in a relationship with me?

As you go through your list, keep an eye out for anything that makes you gasp, grin, or giggle as you think about it...

DAY 2

Goals vs Miracles

'There are two ways to live: you can live as if nothing is
a miracle; you can live as if everything is a miracle.'
ALBERT EINSTEIN

One of the reasons I encourage people to take on 'impossible' projects is that generally speaking, so much more is possible in life than we can imagine with our limited perception. But we are obsessed with being 'realistic.' As one of my students said when I challenged them to actually make their impossible project about what they really, really wanted, 'That would take a miracle.'

But what if miracles aren't as uncommon as we think? Not religious miracles, but the kinds of coincidences, synchronicities, and happy accidents that always seem to be a part of any story of extraordinary success.

Here's the rule of thumb:

**How 'miraculous' something appears is inversely proportional
to how much we think we're at cause in its creation.**

For example, if I write my name on a piece of paper, I'm very unlikely to think of that as a miracle. But if my name appears on the paper seemingly all by itself, that will seem to me to be fairly miraculous. In other words, we tend to attribute anything that comes from a force beyond our own direct actions as being in some sense 'miraculous.'

And this is where the distinction between goals and miracles unveils itself:

If I think it's up to me whether something happens or not, I set it as a goal.

If I think it's up to the universe, I pray (or hope) for a miracle.

Here are a few simple examples:

- If Facebook wants to add another billion dollars to its bottom line, they'll set that as a goal or business objective; if I want to add a billion dollars to mine, I'll pray for a miracle.

- If I want to have an amazing relationship with my kids, I focus on it as a 'goal for the year ahead'; if someone who is deeply estranged from their family wants such a relationship, they hope for a miracle.

- If a doctor wants to cure a patient's life-threatening illness, they put all their energy, attention, and resources into it (treat it as a goal); if a patient's family wants the same result, they may well find themselves praying for a miracle.

What would you like to have happen?

- Make a list of your top three goals for your life, your business, or the world.

- Now make a list of your top three 'miracles' — the three things you would most like to have happen even though you have no idea how or even if they might come about.

Which of these 'miracles' might be fun to engage with as an impossible project for the next 90 days?

DAY 3

Flirt, Date, Engage, Commit

'My wife tricked me into marrying her.
She told me that she liked me.'

McLean Stevenson

Imagine you walk into a bar, not desperate in any way but open to meeting someone wonderful. Your eyes flit over the usual suspects and you flirt with the best of the bunch. One particular someone makes you smile and you decide to go on a date.

The date goes well, so you book another, then another, and eventually you decide to get engaged. After a period of engagement, you're more in love than ever, so you decide to get married.

Now contrast that with the way most people choose a project or goal. They want to jump straight to the end and commit themselves fully to something that may well have just popped into their head a few moments before.

Yet with very few exceptions, people don't ask complete strangers to marry them, don't get engaged without dating first, and don't even go out on a date until at least some form of flirtation has taken place.

That progression – from flirtation to dating to engagement to commitment – is present in the invention of pretty much any future I've seen created over the years by my clients and students. Each stage has its own rewards, and while they can progress as easily over days and weeks as over months and years, there's relatively limited value in trying to jump ahead to commitment without having first put in the hours flirting, dating, and engaging fully in whatever it is you think you might like to be up to.

Spend some time today flirting with a few potential impossible projects. Poke around online, or even 'go on a date' and spend an hour with it as if you'd already decided that project was 'the one.'

If you're more turned on by it after you've spent an hour together, consider taking things to the next level. On Day 6, you'll get the chance to go all the way to commitment...

DAY 4

Ends vs Means

'My best friend is the man who in wishing
me well wishes it for my sake.'
ARISTOTLE

Is your impossible project an end in and of itself or is it a means to that end?

What I mean by that is, is it something that you think is a prerequisite to what you really want, or is it something that you want to create for the simple joy of seeing it come into being?

For example, over the years people have often chosen projects around making a certain amount of money. Sometimes it's for the joy of creating. Often it's because they think it will take the pressure off them or allow them to do something else they'd really like to do but think they can't without money.

Another common project is to lose weight or get fit, but that too can be a means to an end. Do you want to lose weight to prove that you can? Or to impress somebody? Or are you just genuinely excited by the prospect of seeing what you can do with your body as a canvas, or seeing a six pack form on the outside of your stomach for a change?

Remember, the thing itself isn't what makes it a means or an end. Money can be a means or an end. Running a marathon can be a means or an end. Buying a house can be a means or an end. Writing a book can be a means or an end. I remember one of the first books I ever worked on as a ghostwriter back in the early nineties. I asked the person, 'Why do you want a book?' And they said, 'Well, because I think it'll help me reach a wider audience with my business.' What they really wanted was to reach a wider audience. They had no interest in writing a book at all.

The problem with setting up an impossible project as a means to an end is that we're continually having to fill our head with 'motivation' to keep ourselves on track. When our desired end result is actually desired, the motivation will take care of itself.

For the purposes of today, run your impossible project(s) through a simple 'means' test:

Is the end result something that you want to create for the joy and curiosity of seeing it come into being, or is it something you want in order to do something else, to prove something, or to reach an even more desirable end result?

DAY 5

Five Guidelines

*'Once you make a decision, the universe
conspires to make it happen.'*
RALPH WALDO EMERSON

By this point, you hopefully have at least some idea of what you're going to take on for your impossible project. If you're already pretty sure that you know, check it against the five guidelines below:

1. You must believe you have a less than 20 percent chance of success.

A simple rule of thumb is that hard work alone won't be sufficient to complete your project. You want to be in over your head and forced to rely on the invisible giants of inspiration, possibility, and opportunity in order to succeed.

2. You must be sufficiently inspired about what you want to create to be happy to invest time in creating it, regardless of how things turn out.

By definition, you're probably not going to pull this off in the next 90 days. So make sure your impossible project is something you really want to spend a lot of time with over the next few months, regardless of whether or not things work out. Remember, a good rule of thumb is that when you think about it, it makes you gasp, grin, or giggle.

3. Your impossible project should be about creating a result, not a feeling or quality.

Creating results in the world is a manufacturing operation; finding feelings in yourself is essentially a mining operation. Things happen in the outside world through creation, but in the inside world through discovery. This is another way of saying that...

4. It's not about you.

One of the biggest things that will get in the way of creating your impossible project is to turn it into a self-improvement project. This isn't about becoming a better person or overcoming your patterns of self-sabotage and procrastination. It's just about creating stuff in the world, plain and simple.

5. Choose one thing, not 12.

It's so tempting to use the program to attempt to create everything you ever wanted in one go. Unfortunately, that usually turns out to be a fantastic strategy for creating nothing. The good news is, most people report that they make all sorts of mysterious progress on their other projects even while they focus on just one.

If you had to choose your project today, what would it be? What makes you grin, gasp, and/or giggle just to think about it?

DAY 6

Booking Your Sailing to Bombay

'You can, you should, and if you're brave
enough to start, you will.'
STEPHEN KING

One of my all-time favorite quotes is from the Scottish mountaineer W.H. Murray, who wrote:

> *Until one is committed, there is hesitancy, the chance to draw back, always ineffectiveness. Concerning all acts of initiative (and creation), there is one elementary truth, the ignorance of which kills countless ideas and splendid plans: that the moment one definitely commits oneself, then Providence moves too. All sorts of things occur to help one that would never otherwise have occurred. A whole stream of events issues from the decision, raising in one's favour all manner of unforeseen incidents, meetings and material assistance, which no man could have dreamt would have come his way. I learned a deep respect for one of Goethe's couplets:*
>
> *Whatever you can do or dream you can, begin it. Boldness has genius, power and magic in it!*

While I've always found it motivating, I've also used it over the years to beat myself up for having 'commitment issues.' Then one day I actually found a copy of Murray's book *The Scottish Himalayan Expedition* and for the first time read the quote in context:

> *We hadn't really done anything, but when I said that nothing had been done, I erred in one important matter. We had definitely committed ourselves, and were half way out of our ruts. We had put down our passage money, booked*

a sailing to Bombay. This may sound too simple but is great in consequence. Until one is committed, there is hesitancy, the chance to draw back, always ineffectiveness…

I remember reading that and laughing at how I'd used it to turn commitment into an enormous personal development project. All my role model for commitment had actually done at that point was book a sailing to Bombay. Like buying a plane ticket. Like throwing your hat in the ring. Like saying, 'Yeah, I'm in. This is what I'm up to.'

Since that time, commitment hasn't looked like such a difficult thing to me. It's a simple act of declaring what I'm up to – no more, no less.

When you're ready to commit to your impossible project, do something tangible or symbolic as a way of 'booking your sailing to Bombay.' You might like to post it on social media, mark it in your calendar, or get creative and do something you would do if it was really going to happen.

Examples:

- a course participant who wanted to write a book mocked up a cover with their name as author and posted it to social media

- a course leader with an impossible project of winning a bicycle race cancelled their gym membership and booked unlimited training rides at a local spin studio

- a sales team at a financial services company booked their hotel for a celebratory trip after they hit their impossible target

DAY 7

Rest, Review, Recharge, and Renew

'Love makes the impossible possible.'

SYD BANKS

The Week in Review

- I put in the hours on my project:

☐   ☐

Yes   No

- I 'took five':

☐   ☐   ☐   ☐

Not at all   Rarely   Sometimes   Daily

What I did:

....

....

....

....

What I noticed:

. . . .

. . . .

. . . .

. . . .

What happened:

. . . .

. . . .

. . . .

. . . .

WEEK 2

LET THE GAMES BEGIN!

'A journey of a thousand miles begins with a single step.'
LAO TZU

This is where the program really starts. Your mission, should you choose to accept it, will be to show up to and engage with your impossible project each day in whatever way occurs to you, and to respond to what shows up when you do.

To make things easier, I'll put a little reminder at the end of each daily lesson that will ask you four questions:

1. How did you show up to your impossible project today?

2. What did you do?

3. What did you notice?

4. What happened?

You'll find that the simple act of asking and answering these questions each day will help keep you on track and in the game. They'll also prompt the invisible giant of your creative mind to guide you as you go...

IMPOSSIBLE CHALLENGE NO.2:
CREATING FROM NOTHING

Every day this week, you're going to create something from nothing. It might be a piece of writing or a piece of art. It might be a specific conversation with a client or a meal with a friend. It can be related to your impossible project or completely independent of it. The only thing that matters is that by the end of the day each day this week, there will be something tangible in existence that literally did not exist at the beginning of the day.

(If you're using social media for the program, you can share what you've created each day with the #dailycreation.)

DAY 8

The Five Phases of Creation

'Imagination is the beginning of creation.'

GEORGE BERNARD SHAW

This week's impossible challenge is a great opportunity to get a feel for the different phases of the creative process we went through in Chapter 1:

1. You start each day with nothing and you don't have to know what you're going to create before you begin. All you need to know is that you're going to create something today.

2. At some point, something will occur to you and you'll start mucking about with words or paper or music or whatever raw materials are available.

3. Your creation will start to take form and you'll begin to do the work.

4. As you work with it, you may find yourself caught up in the creative flow.

5. At a certain point in the process, you'll declare completion. You'll consider it done. You'll declare 'Ta daa!' and leave it to stand or fall on its own.

By the end of the week, chances are you'll have a much clearer sense of how this all works than you do now, so for today your assignment is simple – begin!

How did you show up to your impossible project today?

What did you do? What did you notice? What happened?

DAY 9

The Nose That Means 'Yes'

*'I had a friend who was a clown. When he died, all
his friends went to the funeral in one car.'*

STEVEN WRIGHT

When I was a drama student, one of my favorite workshops was in clowning. We were each handed a red nose and told that if we chose to put it on, we would be joining a sacred order with only one rule:

> *Whilst wearing the sacred red nose, the answer to any question you are asked is an enthusiastic 'Yes!'*

If they said, 'Can you seduce that woman?', you would go over and seduce that woman.

If they said, 'Can you climb that mountain?', you would climb the mountain.

And if they said, 'Can you swallow nitro-glycerine and blow yourself up?', nitro-glycerine would be swallowed and exploding would ensue.

The point of the exercise was that if you didn't block a creative impulse, something new would be created from it.

 Your mission today, should you choose to accept it, is to put on a real or imaginary clown nose, say 'Yes!' to your own creative impulses, and see what comes of it.

How did you show up to your impossible project today?

What did you do? What did you notice? What happened?

DAY 10

Speaking the Impossible

*'According to most studies, people's number one fear is
public speaking. Number two is death, which means,
to the average person, if you go to a funeral, you're
better off in the casket than doing the eulogy.'*

JERRY SEINFELD

A friend once told me how candles were originally made. What the candlemakers would do was take a wick, dip it in hot wax, and then take it out. And a little bit of the wax would stick.

They would then let it dry and stick it back in the wax and take it out again. And of course more wax would stick because there was more substance to it. It was more solid – it had more surface area.

And then they would let it cool and put it in again.

And each time they would dip the wick, the candle would get more and more solid, more and more tangible, more and more real.

In the same way, each time we speak about what we want, even if we think it's 'impossible,' we are speaking it into being. Because each time we speak about it, it becomes just a little bit more real to us, a little bit more solid. Eventually, it becomes so real that other people can start to see it too. Sometimes they can even see it before we can.

And the clearer and more solid the vision, the easier it becomes to create it in the world.

So here's today's experiment:

- Speak about your impossible project. Describe it out loud, wherever you are. Tell the air, or your cat, or ficus tree, or steering wheel. Go into as much detail as you can, then do it again, and do it again.

  At a certain point, if you're like most people, you'll feel as though the impossible project has begun to take form.

  If you find yourself more bunged up in Thought, you can either let it go and come back to it later or carry on until you come out the other side.

- Go and speak about your impossible project to someone else. It can be someone you know, someone you trust, or even a complete stranger. But talk out loud to another human being rather than just posting on Facebook. Once again, notice how your sense of it shifts as you go.

  (Don't confuse this shift with the swirl of feelings that are likely to happen in your body when you think about speaking about it. In fact, until you have spoken about it to someone else, just assume that whatever you think it's going to be like is probably wrong!)

Once you've actually done it — once you've spoken out loud about your project in the world — it becomes a little bit more tangible and a little bit more possible. In that sense, speaking about your project can be one of the first steps in bringing it to life!

How did you show up to your impossible project today?

What did you do? What did you notice? What happened?

DAY 11

The Possibility Game

'Every artist is unreasonable, because he or she is doing something that hasn't been done before.'

ELI BROAD

Years ago I set myself the impossible project of moving house but was absolutely convinced it couldn't happen. Here's the 'transcript' of a coaching conversation I had in my own head:

Coach Michael (CM): What would you love to create in your life?

Michael the Client (MC): *Great question – I guess I'd love to create a new home, but it just doesn't feel sensible right now.*

CM: Let's save sensible for later. What would need to happen in order for you to create a new home in the next 90 days?

MC: *The next 90 days? That's way too soon! And besides, maybe now isn't the time to be spending extra money. Have you seen the news lately?*

CM: Actually, I haven't, but I have heard the football season is about to kick off. And in any case, you haven't answered my question – what would need to happen in order for you to create a new home in the next 90 days?

MC: *Look, we don't actually need to move – the house we live in now is fine, and it feels greedy to want more.*

CM: Got it. So ... what would need to happen in order for you to create a new home in the next 90 days?

MC: *Okay, what would need to happen is that I'd need to know beyond a shadow of a doubt that we had the money and we wouldn't be creating any new debt, make* *a clear decision about buying vs renting and what to do with our existing home, take into account the kids' schools (since we'd be moving mid-year), find a great place, put in an offer, have it accepted, and sort out the details of the actual move.*

CM: Excellent. Now, what would you need to do in order for all that to happen?

MC: *I don't have time to do anything – I'm busy enough as it is!*

CM: Remember, the question wasn't 'Do you have time?' or 'Is it possible?' or even 'Do you really want to?' The question was simply: 'What would you need to do in order for all that to happen?'

MC: *Okay, so in terms of actions, I'd need to go through the books for the past year and the projections for the next two years. I'd also want to build in a back-up plan in case the projections were off. Then, assuming the numbers all worked, it would be as simple as calling a real estate agent and beginning to look at properties.*

CM: Last question for now – are you going to do that?

MC: *Actually, yes – that doesn't sound anywhere near as hard as I thought it was going to be!*

Within two months, we'd moved into our new home.

To play the possibility game with your impossible project, cycle through these three questions as needed:

- 'What would need to happen in order to...?'
- 'What would I need to do in order to...?'
- 'Am I going to do it?'

How did you show up to your impossible project today?

What did you do? What did you notice? What happened?

DAY 12

Why Not?

'Some men see things as they are, and ask why.
I dream of things that never were, and ask why not?'

ROBERT KENNEDY, QUOTING GEORGE BERNARD SHAW

In 1992, when Bill Clinton was running for president of the United States, he and his team were up against the fact that he was a governor from an obscure southern state and nobody really knew who he was. They needed to do something extraordinary in order to put him on the map.

His campaign managers, James Carville and Paul Begala, decided to stand the normal structure of creative meetings on their head. Instead of doing what is traditional, which is to insist that any idea has to be thoroughly vetted and approved before it can be tried, they decided to do the opposite.

As they felt they were playing a losing hand (and therefore had nothing to lose), they told their people that unless someone could come up with a compelling reason not to do something within an hour of it being proposed, it was automatically approved.

Consequently, instead of the campaign trying one or two new things a week, they were trying 30. So even if 20 of them totally failed, the other 10 would move the needle and create some momentum.

Just for today, make the default for any idea you have to move things forward on your impossible project a resounding 'Why not?' and see what happens!

How did you show up to your impossible project today?

What did you do? What did you notice? What happened?

DAY 13

Someday Is Just a Thought

*'Never doubt that a small group of thoughtful,
committed citizens can change the world;
indeed, it's the only thing that ever has.'*

MARGARET MEAD

My friend and colleague Mara Gleason Olsen is the co-founder, with her husband, Eirik Olsen, of the One Solution Global initiative, a non-profit whose mission is to take the principles behind creating the impossible and share them in a way that takes on the big issues in the world.

Here's her description of the moment the initiative went from 'impossible dream' to reality:

> *Rightly or wrongly, the world in 2016 seemed to be more and more in a fear-driven mode – the threat of terrorism and the seemingly endless instability in the Middle East; racial tensions in America on the rise; Brexit; Trump vs Hillary. Twenty-four-hour media programs were pointing out the suffering, divide and conflict everywhere you looked.*

> *Our field was illuminating a universal set of principles that explained a) where the human experience and feelings actually came from, and b) that we were all using the same basic principles to create our experience, so we were all the same underneath our separate thoughts. Those two facts, if and when understood, made the world immediately more united, stable and hopeful.*

> *As Eirik and I sat on the couch discussing the creation of a conference about global issues, I felt myself getting more and more charged up.*

I said, 'I am so sick of watching the news and seeing all of the struggles of the world and thinking, If only everyone understood the principles, then none of this shit would be happening.

'There's actually a really simple solution. You can't have racism if you know that everything is made of thought. Racism isn't a thing. It's a thought that someone treats as though it's true. Babies aren't racist because they haven't learned to believe that their thinking is correct yet. And you can't have war, because you could never kill someone if you knew that we all lived in our own thought-created separate realities. And to say that mine is right and yours is wrong makes no sense. Blaming someone else or some group of people for "making me" feel something also stops making sense. How could I harm someone if they can't make me feel bad? Even the lines we've drawn around territories and states and countries – they're all made of thought. And then we argue over them as if they somehow exist outside of thought. It's crazy.

'Someday,' I continued, 'everyone will understand these principles and then, and only then, will the world actually experience peace and global security!'

Eirik looked at me, totally deadpan, and said, 'You know that someday is just a thought too. It doesn't exist. It's just an idea. So it never gets any closer.'

And that's when my head exploded.

I realized about 15 things in the flash of a second. One was that time is an illusion. Period. We only experience now. I know people talk about that all the time, and I know I'd glimpsed that notion several times before, but in that moment I felt the truth of it in my entire being.

Someday is made up. It's just a thought. It's not a real thing. Now is all we experience. So, would now be a good time to get your impossible dream out of your head and into the world?

Don't forget to create something from nothing today — to bring something into the world before the day is done that didn't exist in the world when the day began!

How did you show up to your impossible project today?

What did you do? What did you notice? What happened?

DAY 14

Rest, Review, Recharge, and Renew

'The bad news is you're falling through the air – nothing to hang on to, no parachute. The good news is there's no ground.'
CHÖGYAM TRUNGPA

The Week in Review

- I put in the hours on my project:

☐　　　　☐
Yes　　　　No

- I created something from nothing:

☐　　　　☐　　　　☐　　　　☐
Not at all　　Rarely　　Sometimes　　Daily

What I did:

. . . .

. . . .

. . . .

. . . .

What I noticed:

....

....

....

....

What happened:

....

....

....

....

WEEK 3

YOUR INNER GPS

'Sometimes when we pray for guidance,
we're guided in unexpected directions.
We may want a lofty answer and we get
the intuition to clean our bedroom.'

JULIA CAMERON

This week we'll be exploring the role of your inner guidance in creating your impossible project. After all, if you're in uncharted territory, you can't rely on someone else's ideas for how to navigate it. So, you'll learn to look to your own inner sense of knowing, listen to the whispers of the invisible giant, and get a feel for what it is to follow the wisdom within.

As you come to recognize this sense of knowing, it will become one of your most reliable allies as you work through your impossible project. It'll be the compass that guides you when apparently unreasonable ideas and opportunities start to present themselves. Which is — spoiler alert — how the impossible becomes possible over time.

IMPOSSIBLE CHALLENGE NO.3:
LIVING IN BLACK AND WHITE

Live this week according to two guidelines: 'I know what to do' and 'I don't know what to do.'

If you know what to do, do it.

If you don't know what to do, don't do anything.

See what happens...

DAY 15

An Introduction to Inner Knowing

'The reasonable man adapts himself to the world:
the unreasonable one persists in trying to adapt
the world to himself. Therefore all progress
depends on the unreasonable man.'
GEORGE BERNARD SHAW

In March 1999 I had a moment of absolute knowing that I needed to move to America. I remember going home and saying to my wife, 'Hey, how do you feel about living in LA?'

When she said, 'Why?', I realized that I didn't know – I just knew it was the next thing to do.

I'd been living in London for over a decade, and during that time I'd studied, met a girl, married, started a career, and had two children. There was no reason to move, but because I had no reason to justify it, I couldn't be reasoned out of it. I just knew.

And that knowing saw me through all the practical, social, and psychological difficulties of moving my very British family to America.

Our inner sense of knowing is a capacity that we seem to be born with – a kind of pre-verbal instinct that shows up as a felt sense in the body. It's a no-brainer in the sense that we don't have to go to our brain and work it out.

So, what do you know?

You know your name. You probably know where you were born, where you went to school, your marital status, and whether or not you have children. You may know what's on your schedule for the rest of the day. You may even know some things that you shouldn't logically know – what some people would call an intuitive or even psychic form of knowing.

You might not know what time it is. Or what you'll be eating for dinner. You definitely don't know what kind of mood you'll be in when you wake up tomorrow morning.

What you know or don't know isn't so important; what's important is getting a feel for knowing, because it will really help you as you go forward. You'll be able to do what you know is right for you for now, regardless of how you happen to be feeling at the moment, what someone tells you you should do, or how you think things will turn out.

- Think of three times in your life when you just knew what to do (or not to do) and followed through on it.

- Think of three things that you know right now. And three things that you don't know.

- What three things do you know about your impossible project?

Repeat these questions often over the course of this week until you know what your inner sense of knowing feels like in your body. You'll find it to be a reliable guide in every area of your life.

How did you show up to your impossible project today?

What did you do? What did you notice? What happened?

DAY 16

Programming
Your Inner GPS

*'Definiteness of purpose is the starting
point of all achievement.'*

W. Clement Stone

If you've got a smartphone, you'll know they have navigation apps on them. And they give you step by step, turn by turn directions to wherever you want to go. They take into account traffic, they take into account road closures, and they take into account what's going on in real time, because they have access to all that data. You don't need to know any of that. All you need to do is to tell the system where you want to go.

In order to work its magic, your GPS only needs two pieces of data from you: it needs as specific an address as you can give it for where you want to go, and it needs an accurate location of where you are now. And then it calculates the best route, given what is going on in traffic right now.

While your inner GPS doesn't work exactly like a smartphone app, in some ways it actually goes one better, taking into account all sorts of unseen factors that you can't even imagine when you set out.

There are only two things your inner guidance system needs to work as designed:

1. A clear destination

This is the desired end result of your impossible project – whatever it is you want to create. You just need to be able to type that into your GPS.

You can do that by writing it out, speaking it aloud, or (as we'll do on a future day) drawing a picture of it.

Then you can just forget about it. In the same way that you don't need to continually remind your phone's GPS of where it's taking you, as soon as you know where you're headed, you don't need to think about it anymore.

2. Access to your current location

In order for your GPS to be able to locate you, you have to have location services on. It's the same with an inner GPS, but most of us don't have location services on very accurately, because we are continually distorting where we are by judging it.

How does this happen? Let's say that you're working on a project and you need sponsorship for it and I ask you, 'Hey, how's it going with your impossible project?'

And you go, 'Oh my God, it's amazing! I've got this call booked with this guy who can fund the whole project by himself and he seems really interested.'

And I go, 'Oh wow, that's great.'

An hour later I ask, 'Hey, how's it going with your impossible project?'

And you go, 'Oh my God, it's awful. This guy, I was really counting on him for sponsorship, and he turned me down.'

And I go, 'Oh man, that's too bad.'

The relevant question is not 'How's it going?' as in 'How are you feeling about it?' The relevant question is:

'Where are you now in relation to where you ultimately want to be?'

Where am I now? I have got this many calls set up, I have sent this many emails, I have put in this many hours, I am this far along in the project. I am on Week 3, Day 16.

And I know my inner GPS will take care of everything else.

For today, your assignment is simple:

● Write down your 'impossible' destination.

● Write a 'just the facts' statement of where you are now.

Once you have a clear sense of where you're going and where you are now, what will almost always happen is that the next step will emerge.

How do you know it's the next step? It's something that you can and will do today.

How did you show up to your impossible project today?

What did you do? What did you notice? What happened?

DAY 17

Beyond the Word

'If I could sing a song for you, I would sing a song for you. If I could dance for you, I would dance. If I could paint a picture, I would paint. But my thing is words – words. And words are dangerous because you might listen to them. And that would be a mistake.'

ANONYMOUS

Years ago I remember reading a book by Shad Helmstetter called *What to Say When You Talk to Yourself*. The idea was that words had power, and that if you weren't careful with the way you worded your internal dialogue, you would suffer for it.

Similarly, many goal-setting manuals have offered specific rules for how to word your goals for maximum effect, as though the words themselves are magical incantations that will create or block the creation of your desired end result.

Yet in my experience, the language we use to describe what we want to create is far less important than our inner sense of it.

- Today, fold a piece of paper in half vertically.

- On the right–hand side of the page, draw a picture of your impossible project as though it already existed in the world. Your picture can be realistic or symbolic. It does not have to be 'good.'

- On the left–hand side of the page, draw a picture of your current reality. (Here's my example for this book... :–)

● Put the pictures up somewhere where you can see them throughout the day and take action on any inspired next steps that occur to you.

How did you show up to your impossible project today?

What did you do? What did you notice? What happened?

DAY 18

Back from the Future

*'Without leaps of imagination or dreaming, we
lose the excitement of possibilities. Dreaming,
after all, is a form of planning.'*

GLORIA STEINEM

While most planning processes attempt to work forward from present to future, an interesting way to spark your creativity is to work backward from the future to the present...

Imagine you've already created your impossible project...

● What was the very last action you took before declaring 'Ta daa!'?

● What did you do before that?

● And before that?

● And before that?

Keep on tracking back from the future until you come to an action you can take today ... and take it!

How did you show up to your impossible project today?

What did you do? What did you notice? What happened?

DAY 19

There's No Such Thing as a Decision

'Often I had the feeling that in all decisive matters, I was no longer among men, but was alone with God.'

C.G. JUNG

For years I was fascinated by the art of making decisions, as it seemed to me to be at the core of living a productive, contributory life. During that time, I experimented with a number of different decision-making strategies designed to make me less wishy-washy and unleash the power of decision in my world.

Here are just a few of the experiments I tried:

- Making one strong decision a day for a year.

- Flipping a coin and following the flip.

- Starting with a 'no' unless persuaded it was a 'yes.'

- Making each decision either a 'hell, yeah' or a 'no.'

- Writing down 10 decisions a day for 10 days.

- Flipping a coin and noticing which way I hoped it landed.

- Starting with a 'yes' unless persuaded it was a 'no.'

- Taking 'maybe' to mean 'no for now.'

While I did feel more decisive during each of these experiments, I noticed that none of them changed my fundamental feelings of indecisiveness and self-doubt.

When each experiment was over, I went back to equivocating between multiple options and living the majority of my life in what my coach at the time, Steve Hardison, called 'the wobbliness of maybe.'

Then something interesting started to happen. As I learned more about the principle of Thought, I came to see that it was actually natural for things to first look one way and then another. What was unnatural (but incredibly common) was to hang on to one perspective or point of view and pretend that it was the right way to see things and all thoughts to the contrary were just wrong. Therefore the continual 'changing my mind' that I experienced was part of the natural variability of thought, and not, as I had feared, a sign of some flaw in my brain or character.

This raised a new question for me – if I knew that left to its own devices my brain would continually offer me justification for whatever course of action happened to be in front of it at the time (i.e., 'Whatever the thinker thinks, the prover proves'), how could I ever really know what was the best thing to do?

The answer, as so often happens, didn't become obvious to me until I had an insight at a higher level of consciousness:

There's no such thing as a decision.

While we can certainly describe the moment before we embark on a particular course of action as being a 'choice point' and label the taking of the action as 'a decision,' all that's really happening is this:

We're doing things and thinking about a) whether or not we should be doing them and b) whether or not we'd be better off doing different things.

In other words, but for our thinking, we're just doing some things and not others every given moment of our life. The only times we even notice what seems like a decision is when the natural flow of thought gets interrupted. Then we start thinking about what might happen, for better or for worse, if we do or don't take an action, and we take that thinking to heart as if it's significant or even crucial to our wellbeing.

If we label the feeling of that thinking as 'being indecisive,' we think the 'solution' to that feeling must be to 'make a decision.' But in reality, we navigate the vast majority of our life without any real awareness of the navigational process. Personal thoughts and apparent decisions come and go, while we continue happily forward from a 'no-brainer' place of deeper knowing. From this place – deeper thought coming directly from a deeper intelligence and wisdom that guides our actions – we have the experience of living in an easy flow of choiceless choices and decisionless decisions.

Here's a simple experiment:

 For the rest of today, live as if there's no such thing as a decision. Any time you don't know what to do, don't do anything. Allow your thoughts to come and go as they please. See what happens.

How did you show up to your impossible project today?

What did you do? What did you notice? What happened?

DAY 20

'Don't Be a Moron'

'Common sense is genius dressed in working clothes.'
RALPH WALDO EMERSON

I was having lunch with a friend who'd survived a heart attack a couple of years earlier. When I asked him if he had any dietary restrictions, he shared the story of going to his doctor post-coronary with a written list of questions about what he should and shouldn't eat going forward.

The doctor took a look at the list, then ripped it up and threw it in the bin.

'Here's my dietary advice,' he said. 'Don't be a moron.'

'What do you mean?' asked my friend.

'I mean,' replied the doctor, 'use your common sense. Eat heart-healthy food most of the time, and if you really fancy the odd bowl of macaroni and cheese, enjoy it.'

While I was a little taken aback at the bluntness of the advice when I first heard the story, I've come to realize that it's a fantastic response for pretty much any kind of question people have about how to live their lives.

For example, when Dr. Roger Mills and his team went to introduce the inside-out understanding into the Modello and Homestead Gardens housing projects in Florida, known to be home base for a number of gang members and drug dealers, his safety instructions to his colleagues were 'Just use your common sense.' This is, of course, the polite way of saying 'Don't be a moron.'

Not only was no one on his staff harmed, but within three years the drug trafficking and serious crime rate in the community had dropped to zero. (You can read more about this amazing story in the book *Modello: A Story of Hope for the Inner City and Beyond* by Jack Pransky.)

Similarly, one of the most common concerns expressed by people in my private practice is that if they begin to live more in their innate wellbeing and allow their deeper wisdom to guide their lives, it will somehow lead to massive financial irresponsibility, complete apathy, or even the abandonment of their families. As the results are invariably the exact opposite, I sometimes use the following analogy to address their concerns:

> *Imagine you buy a new car that has a GPS system pre-installed. You are enjoying getting a feel for how the car drives and how much easier it is to simply be guided by the GPS than to have to pre-plan your route.*
>
> *After a time, the GPS tells you to take a left turn ahead. When you look, there is a large brick building exactly where the nav system is telling you to go.*
>
> *Do you a) crash your car into the brick building, or b) stick on the main road and wait for the nav system to recalculate your route?*

In other words, just because you begin to rely on a real-time, highly responsive navigational system doesn't mean that you suddenly become a moron.

The design of the human system seems to be that our common sense and deeper wisdom work best when used together. The wisdom of our deeper mind guides our way forward whenever we let it, without ever trying to take away our free will. And the more we come to rely on that deeper wisdom to guide us, the more we'll start to notice our common sense coming to the fore whenever we need it most.

How did you show up to your impossible project today?

What did you do? What did you notice? What happened?

DAY 21

Rest, Review, Recharge, and Renew

'If you can't, you won't.'

RICHARD BANDLER

The Week in Review

- I put in the hours on my project:

  ☐
  Yes

  ☐
  No

- If I knew what to do, I did it. If I didn't, I didn't do anything:

  ☐
  Not at all

  ☐
  Rarely

  ☐
  Sometimes

  ☐
  Daily

  What I did:

  ....

  ....

  ....

  ....

What I noticed:

....

....

....

....

What happened:

....

....

....

....

WEEK 4

LEARNING TO FAIL

If you want to succeed, double your failure rate.

THOMAS J. WATSON SR, FORMER PRESIDENT OF IBM

This week's theme is failure — why it is that we've learned to make such a big deal out of things not working. It's important because the most common reason why people don't get anywhere is that they give up before they start, or they take themselves out of the game before they've ever really gotten into it.

On the whole, they give up in the present to avoid feeling bad in the future. But, as we've already learned, our feelings only come from our thinking, and failing to create a specific result in a particular time-frame can't make us feel a way we don't think...

IMPOSSIBLE CHALLENGE NO.4: BREAKING THE RULES

Each day this week, do something that goes against 'the rules of the game.' Ask for a massive discount at a retail store, order pizza in a Chinese restaurant, sing a song in public and pass the hat for money, or initiate a conversation with a stranger. See what happens.

Chances are, your head won't explode, and you may even wind up with a discount, a pizza, and an interesting conversation or two...

DAY 22

Trial and Success

'There is no greater mistake than to try
to leap an abyss in two jumps.'
DAVID LLOYD GEORGE

Anyone who has had a child (or, for that matter, been one) knows that toddlers don't learn to walk and talk in order to impress their mummy and daddy. They learn to walk in order to get somewhere they want to be faster than they can do it by butt-shuffling or crawling, and they learn to speak in order to request milk or food or more of whatever it is they want more of.

But soon the innate curiosity and satisfaction of the learning process get distorted by positive and negative reinforcement. In our desire to be liked, appreciated, and rewarded for everything we do, we then try to avoid the 'error' part of the equation and not make any mistakes.

Since it's impossible to learn anything new without making dozens, hundreds, or even thousands of mistakes, depending on the complexity of the task, the easiest way to avoid it is not to attempt it, or to attempt it so tentatively that it's obvious to everyone around us that we aren't really trying, so can't be held accountable for our lack of success.

But here's the thing: we were made to learn through experimentation — trial and error; trial and success.

Self-consciousness is the number one enemy of this natural kind of learning and, by proxy, the number one enemy of what it's possible for us to achieve. So how can we bring our natural curiosity and desire to learn back to life and set it loose to help us create our most impossible projects and goals?

By getting ourselves out of the way.

'We' are just a collection of habitual thoughts anyway. 'We' are a character in the play of life, and chances are we chose some aspects of our character very carefully without noticing that 'the kind of person we are' is all made up.

Just for today, take on at least one task that you're pretty sure you're going to fail at.

Stay out of your head about it as best you can. When you hear the voices of doom in your mind or feel the feeling of impending disaster in your body, swipe left. (I'm assured this is a culturally relevant reference to getting rid of something you aren't attracted to and don't want to spend time with.)

Do it. Fail. Get it wrong.

Then, when you're ready, do it again.

Repeat as needed.

How did you show up to your impossible project today?

What did you do? What did you notice? What happened?

DAY 23

Thinking about Thinking about Failure

*'Our greatest weakness lies in giving up. The most
certain way to succeed is to try just one more time.'*
THOMAS EDISON

There's a glass elevator near to the venue where I often teach in Los Angeles. When you first get into the elevator, you're at street level and you're staring at concrete. Then you go up a little higher and you can see the hotel across the street. At a certain point, you get to a level where you can see the mountains. And then you get higher and you can see the ocean.

And it's quite incredible, because when you're down at the bottom there's no clue that you're going to have that view up at the top.

If you step aboard the glass elevator in relation to your thinking, you'll notice that there are four distinct levels of understanding thought. And each one of those levels will help you relate to your thinking about failure in a different way...

Ground floor: 'My thoughts are indicative of who I am'

When you look at thought from near the bottom of the elevator, it really seems as though who you are is just the fruit of your thinking. If you have anxious thoughts, you're probably an anxious person; if you have happy thoughts, you must be a happy person.

But what's missed at this level is that you are not your thinking. You're the space inside which the thoughts come and go. And when you start to see that, that takes you a little higher in the elevator...

Lower floors: 'My thoughts are like the weather'

When thought starts to seem like the weather, it stops seeming like a good idea to try to control it moment by moment.

Having said that, most of us still spend an awful lot of time thinking about the weather, and taking the weather into account, and trying to predict the weather, and planning what we will do or won't do with our time, based on the forecast for the week ahead.

But if you travel further up the elevator, you may find...

Upper floors: 'My thoughts are like a dream'

The great thing about dreams is that when they're done, you get to wake up and get on with your life as if nothing happened. You can be on a grand adventure with wizards and dragons and have love affairs with glamorous stars and starlets and die in a blaze of glory all alone at the bottom of a well, and then just wake up to reality without ever having to deal with the imaginary consequences of your imaginary actions.

On the whole, we know that what happens in our head when we sleep doesn't really need to be dealt with on the physical plane. But some of us still analyze our dreams. We search for hidden meanings. Some of us will even go through rituals to create more positive dreams and avoid nightmares.

And so, even when thought looks like a waking dream it still leaves us with preferences for one kind of thinking and experience over another. And so our head is still filled up with trying to do something about our thinking, which limits our access to the deeper clarity, guidance, wisdom and wellbeing that allows us to create the impossible.

But continue on up to the top floor with a view of the ocean and you'll see...

Top floors: 'My thoughts are like a shadow'

When people really reflect on the infinite variability of Thought and the constant Consciousness inside which the game of life plays itself out, then our individual thoughts start to look like mere fluctuations in energy and form. They may seem beautiful or ugly, but no more significant than reflections in a kaleidoscope, dust particles under a microscope, or shadows in a shaded playground.

And because most of us get that every shadow is just a side-effect of light, we don't tend to spend much time studying individual shadows. We don't waste our energy reading meaning into their presence or absence, or trying to avoid the bad shadows and create good ones. Better still, when our thinking appears to us as an ephemeral series of random shadows, our eye is drawn more and more to the light that creates them.

In the same way, when you see that the feeling of failure is made of thought and thought is as temporary as a shadow, it stops looking significant or scary. There's no need to do anything in particular to avoid it. Best of all, fear of failure stops looking like a good reason to do or not do anything.

How did you show up to your impossible project today?

What did you do? What did you notice? What happened?

DAY 24

How to Win the Mental Game

'One caution about "the zone": it cannot be controlled.'

W. Timothy Gallwey

One of my godsons is ranked in the top 10 tennis players aged 10 or under in southern California. The only real weakness in his game, as best I can tell, is that from time to time he lets his frustration get the better of him, to the point of breaking down in tears during a match. When his parents asked me if I could have a talk with him about it, I was both delighted and a bit daunted. How do you talk about the keys to great performance with a nine year old?

We took my dog for a walk on the long dirt access road in the hills near where we live, and as the three of us crested the first hill, I asked him if his parents had told him why we were having a talk.

'It's because my mental game needs work, Mikey,' he said, in language that sounded way more sophisticated than I was expecting. 'Sometimes I get really mad at myself if I make an unforced error, and then I make even more mistakes.'

I asked him if he ever made unforced errors without getting upset, or got upset with himself when he was winning. He said, 'No,' at first, but then started to remember instances of both.

'So, if it's not the unforced errors and it can happen even when things are going well, what do you think it really is that frustrates you?' I asked.

At that moment, a large pickup truck came barrelling down the road, kicking up a dust cloud that enveloped us. While the dog seemed unperturbed, my godson and I covered our faces and an idea occurred to me.

'Let's wait here and see what happens to the dust,' I said.

We did, and of course within a minute or so it was as if the truck had never been there.

'That dust is a lot like the frustration,' I said. 'If you don't try to do anything with it, it will settle back down all by itself.'

We walked on, and several other cars and trucks drove by, some kicking up clouds of dust and some barely bringing up any dust at all.

'Those cars are like thoughts in our head,' I said. 'Some of them bring up a lot of dust, and some just pass by without our really noticing.'

I saw his eyes light up a bit. 'So can you show me how to stop the cars that make the dust?'

'No, buddy — it doesn't really work that way. We don't get to decide which cars come, or when they come, or even how many of them are driving down the road today.'

He seemed disappointed, and I carried on.

'Now imagine that you could stop one of the cars when it drove by, and you made the driver drive back and forth over the same bit of road. What would happen?'

'Big dust!' he said, the twinkle returning to his eyes.

'That's right. And that's what it's like when we keep thinking about the same thing and running over it in our mind again and again.'

'So, if I can't control the cars or the dust,' he asked, 'how am I going to stop getting so frustrated?'

I thought for a moment. 'When you're playing really good tennis, do you think about how you're feeling?'

'Not really. I sometimes think about which side of the court to hit to or whether to come up to the net, but mostly I just play.'

'That's right,' I said. 'That's why you don't have to try to stop the cars. You just play tennis. Everything else will take care of itself.'

At that point we turned off the road and onto a hiking trail.

'And the cool thing is,' I added, 'when you play against people who are better than you, you usually get better. Losing doesn't mean anything about you — you're OK either way.'

'I know,' he said, once again sounding like someone who was much wiser than his years.

I know that win or lose, he will be OK. He always has been. And regardless of our own history of victories and defeats, the same is true for all of us.

How would you approach your impossible project if you knew that you didn't have to feel great to do great?

How would you approach your impossible project if you knew that you didn't have to take it seriously to do a seriously good job?

How did you show up to your impossible project today?

What did you do? What did you notice? What happened?

DAY 25

Three Questions

*'Success is stumbling from failure to failure
with no loss of enthusiasm.'*

WINSTON CHURCHILL

In over 25 years as a coach, I've come to see that the problem is rarely that people don't know what to do to follow their goals and dreams. The problem is that they're scared to do it in case it doesn't work out.

So here are some questions designed to spark your creative mind into generating some action steps for your impossible project. Each one addresses this week's theme of the gap between what we do, how we feel about what we do, and just how much more freedom we have to act when we're less worried about how we feel...

- What would you do to move your project forward if you didn't have to feel bad about it no matter how things worked out?

- What would you do to enroll other people in your project if you weren't afraid of failing?

- What would you attempt if you knew you *couldn't* fail?

 Take some time to reflect on these questions and any others that come to mind throughout the day and then act on what you see!

How did you show up to your impossible project today?

What did you do? What did you notice? What happened?

DAY 26

Do the Thing

'I did stand-up comedy for 18 years – ten of those years were spent learning, four years were spent refining, and four years were spent in wild success. The course was more plodding than heroic.'

STEVE MARTIN

One of my favorite essays is 'On Compensation' by Ralph Waldo Emerson. Here's an excerpt that's extremely relevant to creating the impossible:

> *...in labor as in life there can be no cheating. The thief steals from himself. The swindler swindles himself. For the real price of labor is knowledge and virtue, whereof wealth and credit are signs. These signs, like paper money, may be counterfeited or stolen, but that which they represent, namely, knowledge and virtue, cannot be counterfeited or stolen. These ends of labor cannot be answered but by real exertions of the mind, and in obedience to pure motives. The cheat, the defaulter, the gambler, cannot extort the knowledge of material and moral nature which his honest care and pains yield to the operative.*

> *The law of nature is, Do the thing, and you shall have the power; but they who do not the thing have not the power.*

There is something right now that you know you're not doing. If you did it, your impossible project would come 20 miles closer today. But you don't. You don't because you don't know how. You don't because it's too hard. You don't because you don't want to fail. You don't because, well, you're just not the kind of person who does things like that.

But, according to Emerson, the law of nature is that if you do the thing, you'll have the power. That's about 180 degrees from the way people tell us it works. They say that you have to be able to do it before you can do it, but in fact it's when you do it that you develop the ability to do it. Start walking and falling, and getting up, and walking and falling, and getting up, and you will develop the ability to walk across the room.

Your assignment today is to find the one thing that you could do that would make the biggest positive difference to your impossible project ... and do it.

It's fine if you do it badly. It's fine if you're terrified as you do it. It's even fine if you hate me and curse my name as you do it.

But what you'll find is that as you do it, it gets easier and easier to do.

How did you show up to your impossible project today?

What did you do? What did you notice? What happened?

DAY 27

Infinite Possibilities

*'We don't create abundance. Abundance is
always present. We create limitation.'*
ARNOLD PATENT

One of the participants in a group I was leading presented a seemingly intractable dilemma concerning their job. When I asked them if they'd be willing for the situation to change, they said, 'Yes,' but then went on to explain why it couldn't.

The reason I knew they were wrong, without having to know anything about their job or personal history, is that there's no such 'thing' as a 'situation' — we create 'situations' via the principles of Thought and Consciousness.

Thought is the principle behind creation — the infinite play dough that makes up the world we see around us. It's the film strip that creates the specific version of the world we think is real out of the infinite possible versions waiting to be created.

Consciousness is the principle behind awareness — the light that brings our thinking to life and the movie screen that allows us to experience the projections of the mind as if they're happening to us instead of coming from us.

Together, Thought and Consciousness create the illusion of a fixed, unchanging reality. We can see and feel what looks like the edge of the world and even point to the dragons who live there. After all, everyone knows a story about someone who started getting ideas above their station and wound up being swallowed alive.

Yet what about the times we've stepped over the edge of our world and survived? Did we just get lucky, or could it be that 'edges' only exist in the limited world of our own imagination?

After a bit of exploration of the illusory nature of our thought-created limitations, I asked the participant a second question: 'Are you open to finding new ways to make money?'

While you might think that's an easy enough question to answer, it completely stumped them. In fact, I was only able to get an answer (after multiple attempts) when I wrote the question on the board and offered a simple multiple choice:

a) Yes.

b) No.

Much to all our surprise, the answer they circled was 'No.'

Bizarre as that may seem at first glance, think about it for yourself. Where in your life are you bumping up against the limitations created by your own imagination? Where do you think you already know what's possible and what's not? In what area or areas of your life are you trying to order off a limited menu, unaware that there's a chef in the kitchen waiting to whip up something brand new if only you'd put in the order?

It's what we think we know that holds us back; it's what we're open to being wrong about that opens up a wider world. And this is the key to expanding into the natural abundance of possibility that surrounds us:

When we open our mind to seeing something new, we inevitably see something new.

Here's a simple experiment to see this more clearly for yourself:

● Ask yourself a series of 'Am I willing...?' questions until you bump into the edge of your world. You'll know you've hit it because the answer to that question won't be an unqualified, no-brainer 'Yes.'

Examples:

− 'Am I willing to succeed?'

− 'Am I willing to succeed at...?'

– 'Am I willing to love what I do?'

– 'Am I willing to love what I am doing now?'

– 'Am I willing to be happy and content without anything in my life changing?'

● Once you've bumped into the edge, ask yourself if you're open to seeing something new beyond it. This may be more difficult than you expect, as most of us aren't really open to being wrong about the way we currently see 'reality.'

Once you've opened up to seeing something new, prepare for your reality to change...

How did you show up to your impossible project today?

What did you do? What did you notice? What happened?

DAY 28

Rest, Review, Recharge, and Renew

'Ever tried? Ever failed? No matter.
Try again. Fail again. Fail better.'
SAMUEL BECKETT

The Week in Review

- I put in the hours on my project:

  ☐   ☐

  Yes   No

- I broke the rules:

  ☐   ☐   ☐   ☐

  Not at all   Rarely   Sometimes   Daily

What I did:

....

....

....

....

What I noticed:

....

....

....

....

What happened:

....

....

....

....

WEEK 5

CREATING MOMENTUM

*'At a certain point you can't
really tell if you have created
the momentum or it's creating you.'*
ANNIE LENNOX

Sometimes people are inclined to give up early on their impossible project because of how hard it is and how little reward they seem to be getting for the effort they're putting in. Momentum reverses this ratio, creating the experience of seemingly effortless productivity and even at times a sense of destiny. This week we're going to be exploring different ways that you can generate momentum on your impossible project.

Until a project reaches its tipping point, inertia makes it easier to stop than keep going; once it reaches its tipping point, it's easier to keep going than to stop.

While you may have to put in the hours to get the ball rolling, after a time the ball will be rolling so fast that the hardest part of the job will be keeping up. As your project takes on a life of its own, you'll discover that what seemed really impossible when it was all down to you is actually not impossible at all...

IMPOSSIBLE CHALLENGE NO. 5:
ONE HUNDRED ACTIONS

This week, your impossible challenge is to take and track 100 actions toward the realization of your impossible project.

What counts as an action is up to you, but essentially, if it's designed to move your project forward, it counts, whether it 'works' or not!

(You can track your hundred actions using the chart on day 35!)

DAY 29

The Flywheel of Creation

'Sometimes your creative energy is like water in a kinked hose, and before thoughts can flow on the topic at hand, you have to straighten the hose by attending to whatever is preoccupying you.'

NATALIE GOLDBERG

One of the things that can make a project seem impossible is the assumption that 'If it's to be, it's up to me.' Trying to complete your project all on your own, without momentum, is like trying to walk barefoot down a dry riverbed with a canoe balanced on your head. It can sometimes be done, and if you're tough enough and you're hard enough, you may well make it to wherever it is you're heading. But your feet are probably going to be pretty bloody and you're probably going to be exhausted. And very wary of taking on anything big next time.

Moving forward with momentum is waiting for the riverbed to fill with flowing water, taking the canoe off your head, climbing aboard and starting to paddle. You're still fully engaged in your project, but the river is doing most of the work.

Here's another analogy, adapted from the work of management consultant Jim Collins:

> *Imagine a giant flywheel, as heavy and wide and thick as 10 men. That flywheel is your impossible project. Your job is to get it to move as fast as possible because momentum (mass x velocity) is what will generate superior results over time.*

> *At the start of your project, the flywheel is at a standstill. To get it moving, you need to make a tremendous effort. You push with all your might and finally you get the flywheel to inch forward.*

After two or three days of sustained effort, you get the flywheel to complete one entire turn.

You keep pushing and the flywheel begins to move a bit faster. It takes a lot of work, but at last the flywheel makes a second rotation.

You keep pushing steadily. It makes three turns, four turns, five, six.

With each turn, it moves faster, and then at some point – you can't say exactly when – you break through. The momentum of the heavy wheel kicks in. It spins faster and faster with its own weight propelling it. You aren't pushing any harder, but the flywheel is accelerating, its momentum building, its speed increasing...

Momentum is the ultimate force multiplier for success.

● Think about a place in life where you see the power of momentum in action. It can be a specific story from your own life, a time when, at a certain point, a project or goal or process started to take on a life of its own, or it can just be an area of life where you really see, 'Oh my gosh, momentum is a big player here.'

● Ask yourself, 'How do I create momentum in my impossible project so that I'm not doing all the work?'

● Throughout the day, reflect on how momentum may already be showing up around your impossible project.

How did you show up to your impossible project today?

What did you do? What did you notice? What happened?

DAY 30

The Momentum Formula

'Start where you are... Do what you can.'

ARTHUR ASHE

A couple of years ago, I was thumbing through a copy of Dave Ramsey's *EntreLeadership* and randomly opened it to a page that contained a 'theorem' that explained why:

> *...momentum [in business] is not a random lightning strike, but on the contrary it is actually created ... and here is the formula:*

$$Fi/T(G) = M$$

I immediately interpreted the symbols like this:

Focused Intention/Time × 'God' = Momentum

(In Ramsey's actual formula, the 'Fi' stands for 'focused intensity.' I highly recommend reading his book to learn more about his idea.)

What I love about this 'momentum formula' is that it accounts for pretty much everything I've seen created (or not created) in all the years I've been doing this work:

- Enough focused intention over a long enough period of time will accomplish most goals with or without any extra help from the Universal Mind, although whether it really sets the flywheel of momentum spinning seems to be a bit more hit or miss.

- Focused intention plus a bit of help from the energy and intelligence behind life can take us outside the apparent boundaries of time, and sometimes things inexplicably 'just happen' without our putting in anywhere near as much time or effort as we were expecting.

- People who put their faith in the unfolding of life over time without any particular focused intention often wind up with lives of great import and impact, carried by the momentum of what seems to outside eyes as random chance and extreme good fortune.

Of course, when we do put it all together, we maximize our odds of success. When we focus our intention on what it is we want to create in the world, maintain that focus over time, and make space in our mind for previously unseen possibilities while making space in our life for previously unseen opportunities, momentum (and the results that inevitably follow on from its creation) will be ours.

How did you show up to your impossible project today?

What did you do? What did you notice? What happened?

DAY 31

Taking Massive Action

'Intensity clarifies. It creates not only momentum, but also the pressure you need to feel either friction, or fulfillment.'

MARCUS BUCKINGHAM

The CEO of an international non-profit I worked with was a huge fan of the motivational author and speaker Tony Robbins. We got into a conversation one day about what specifically Robbins meant when he talked about 'taking massive action' being a key to success. We explored the question for close to an hour, then, to my amusement, decided that 'massive' meant '20,' and that in order for something to qualify as an 'action' it had to involve making a specific action request of another person.

An action request is exactly what it sounds like – a request that someone take an action on your behalf or on behalf of the project you are working on. So that could include asking a potential customer to buy your product, a museum to display your art, a producer to listen to your music or watch your film, or a client to give you a referral. The essential element is simply that your request, if accepted, engages the other person in your world in some way and/or moves your project forward.

What surprised me was how quickly 'taking massive action' in this way generated momentum. Within a week, my client had made over 100 action requests and received positive responses to more than half of them. Within three months, his organization had tripled its fundraising numbers for the previous year.

Over time, I've played with variations on this idea, both with clients and for myself. Here are some of the ways that seem to make a relatively big difference in a relatively short space of time:

- Making 20 action requests and/or connecting with 20 people per day (in this case, in relation to your impossible project).

- Blazing through 20, 50, or even 150 action steps as quickly as possible.

- Setting aside a significant chunk of your day (and/or night) to make headway and get things moving.

- Taking on the one *huge* obstacle that's been halting your progress.

Today, write down every action request you make in relation to your impossible project. Don't worry about the size of your requests, whether people say 'yes' or 'no,' or even whether they get back to you.

If you repeat this every day for a week, you'll be amazed by what happens. The combined weight of 1,000 tiny snowflakes can create an avalanche of momentum in your project and in your world.

How did you show up to your impossible project today?

What did you do? What did you notice? What happened?

DAY 32

An Overwhelming Bit of Advice

'Our biggest fear is not that we're inadequate. Our biggest fear is that we're powerful beyond measure.'

MARIANNE WILLIAMSON

In his book *The Story of You*, my friend Steve Chandler shares the story of a piece of advice he gave a client who was struggling with what seemed to them to be a huge problem. I'm adapting it here, with his permission, as I think it applies beautifully to creating momentum with your impossible project:

'Do you want to reach your impossible goal?'

'Well, yeah, that's why we're working together. Do you know how I can do it?'

'Sure, I know how you can do it.'

'Well, how?'

'Overwhelm it.'

'What?'

'Overwhelm it.'

'Well, what exactly do you mean by that?'

'Well, take massive action from a wild high-energy state that dwarfs the goal and overwhelms it. Be inappropriate to the goal.'

'You want me to be inappropriate?'

'I do.'

'In what way?'

'Don't take the appropriate amount of action. Take action that is absurdly disproportionate to the goal. Embarrass the goal. Knock it out of the universe. Smash it, slaughter it, and atomize it with crushing action. Go crazy on it. Beat it to a pulp. That's my advice.'

How much more fun could you have if you decided that you were bigger than your goal? How could you overwhelm it?

If you absolutely had to successfully complete your impossible project before the end of 90 days, what three steps would you immediately take?

Take them today and repeat the process as often as you like!

How did you show up to your impossible project today?

What did you do? What did you notice? What happened?

DAY 33

The Big Ask

'You can't ask authentically and gracefully without truly being able to accept "No" for an answer. Because if you're not truly willing to accept "No" for an answer, you're not really asking, you're demanding – you're begging.'

AMANDA PALMER

I got a call once from a client who was a professional comedian. He'd been playing small clubs for most of his career, but a successful show at the Edinburgh Festival Fringe and a couple of television appearances had brought him to the attention of a promoter who'd booked him to play a 3,000-seat auditorium.

He called because he wanted me to fly out and be on call to help him prepare for what would be the biggest gig of his career.

To his surprise, I declined.

'You don't need me there,' I pointed out. 'You just need to stop taking the thought "This is a big gig" so seriously.'

Try this experiment:

● Write down three numbers – a small number, a medium-sized number, and a large number.

● Now imagine that each of these numbers represents an amount of money you need to ask for.

● Which would be the easiest?

● Which would be the hardest?

Nearly everyone who does this experiment says that asking for the small amount of money would be considerably easier than making 'the big ask.' But what they don't see is that they made up these numbers in their own head. They decided what was small, medium, and large. I've had people's small numbers range from less than one to 10,000, and the large number range from 100 to over 100 million.

In other words, we make up how big a deal something is and then act accordingly.

In the world of fundraising, there are two kinds of request. The more common are the many small ways in which people can donate to a cause, but more momentum is created by what is known as 'the big ask.' In any arena, there are usually a few donors who are considered high-influence, high-net-worth individuals. Whole strategies are developed to approach those people and request a big donation. To make the big ask.

How might things be different if we didn't have to weigh up the size of our requests before making them?

For today, I want you to think about what the big ask might be for your impossible project. What action request would create massive momentum, either taking care of everything in one go or getting the ball rolling at a rate and speed that would make the successful completion of the project inevitable?

What would you do if it wasn't a big ask, but a simple request?

Of course, if you want to really create momentum today, you can just go ahead and ask it!

How did you show up to your impossible project today?

What did you do? What did you notice? What happened?

DAY 34

The Tortoise and the Hare

'Discipline is remembering what you want.'
DAVID CAMPBELL

While most of the days this week point to the effectiveness of generating momentum through massive effort, it's worth remembering that sometimes slow and steady wins the race. Here's a story you probably know — Aesop's fable *The Hare and the Tortoise*:

> The Hare was once boasting of his speed before the other animals. 'I have never yet been beaten,' said he, 'when I put forth my full speed. I challenge anyone here to race with me.'
>
> The Tortoise said quietly, 'I accept your challenge.'
>
> 'That is a good joke,' said the Hare. 'I could dance round you all the way.'
>
> 'Keep your boasting till you've beaten me,' answered the Tortoise. 'Shall we race?'
>
> So a course was fixed and a start was made.
>
> The Hare darted almost out of sight at once, but soon stopped and, to show his contempt for the Tortoise, lay down to have a nap.
>
> The Tortoise plodded on and plodded on, and when the Hare awoke from his nap, he saw the Tortoise was near the winning-post and he couldn't run up in time to save the race.
>
> Then said the Tortoise: 'Plodding wins the race.'

Now, if the Tortoise is to be believed, he won the race because he 'plodded' (literally, 'proceeded in a tediously slow manner'). But people who are successful rarely understand the true cause of their success.

While it may be true that the Tortoise did indeed plod, he also did a few other things that may well have contributed more to his victory than he realized...

1. He stayed focused on his goal, not himself

One of the unspoken truths we've been exploring throughout this book is that it's considerably easier to create when it doesn't become about you. That is, staying the course or reaching your goal is best done by actually focusing on the *goal*, not on what success or failure would mean about *you*.

Had the Hare come to one of my seminars, or even worked with me as a private client, I would no doubt have pointed out to him that it's easier to just win a race than it is to win a race *in order to prove you are the fastest animal in the world.*

We often believe that our value and worth in the world are dependent on our performance. In fact, our value and worth in the world are a given, and have nothing to do with what we do or don't do with our life. No amount of success or failure will make us any more or less worthy of love and respect.

2. He kept on going until the race was done

I don't know if the Tortoise actually believed he could win the race when he started out, but somehow he knew he should focus on what was within his control – bringing a disciplined approach to the race and keeping his feet moving until the finish line was crossed.

Although I was born too late to ever watch him play, I used to delight in stories about the tough-mindedness and will to win of Detroit Lions quarterback Bobby Layne. Perhaps my favorite quote about him came from his college teammate Doak Walker, who said, 'Bobby never lost a game – sometimes, he just ran out of time.'

While some might point to the Hare's last-ditch effort to cross the finish line first as showing 'determination,' I would say it was just a desperate attempt to stave off the embarrassment of losing a race to a Tortoise.

Are you approaching your impossible project like the Hare, running around keeping busy so you can prove how good you are at it?

Or are you more like the Tortoise, aware of but unconcerned by your ever-changing moods, focused on what you want to create (not what you think it means about you), and willing to carry on all the way to the end of the race?

How did you show up to your impossible project today?

What did you do? What did you notice? What happened?

DAY 35

Rest, Review, Recharge, and Renew

*'Even if you're on the right track, you'll
get run over if you just sit there.'*

WILL ROGERS

The Week in Review

- I put in the hours on my project:

  ☐   ☐

  Yes   No

- I took and tracked ____ actions toward the realization of my project:

1	2	3	4	5	6	7	8	9	10
11	12	13	14	15	16	17	18	19	20
21	22	23	24	25	26	27	28	29	30
31	32	33	34	35	36	37	38	39	40
41	42	43	44	45	46	47	48	49	50

51	52	53	54	55	56	57	58	59	60
61	62	63	64	65	66	67	68	69	70
71	72	73	74	75	76	77	78	79	80
81	82	83	84	85	86	87	88	89	90
91	92	93	94	95	96	97	98	99	100

What I did:

. . . .

. . . .

. . . .

. . . .

What I noticed:

. . . .

. . . .

. . . .

. . . .

What happened:

....

....

....

....

WEEK 6

A QUESTION OF CONTROL

'If you don't like the way the world is, you change it. You just do it one step at a time.'

MARIAN WRIGHT EDELMAN

One of life's great myths is that if we only try hard enough and do all the right things, we can guarantee success. But the reality of life is more like a game of chess. We are neither in control of the game nor are we at the mercy of it. And anyone can learn to play.

However, as we advance confidently in the direction of our dreams, we begin to discover that the energy and intelligence behind life seems to work with us along the way, unleashing, as W.H. Murray said, 'all manner of unforeseen incidents, meetings and material assistance, which no man could have dreamt would have come his way.' It's 100 percent reliable, even if the way it turns up is 98 percent unpredictable.

IMPOSSIBLE CHALLENGE NO.6:
THE UNSEEN HAND

This week we'll be exploring that unseen hand behind life and seeing how much easier it is to create something when we stop trying to be in charge of the process and let it take over.

So your challenge is to take your hands off the wheel of your project and see what happens. If it occurs to you to do something to move things forward, do it; if nothing occurs to you, do nothing.

Throughout the week, just notice all the possibilities that occur to you and all the opportunities that show up in your world. See if you can spot the creative intelligence of Mind at work behind the scenes...

DAY 36

51 Percent

'You should never bet against anything in science
at odds of more than about 1,012 to 1.'
ERNEST RUTHERFORD

Last year I had an amazing conversation with Bill Goldstein, one of the pioneers in the sports marketing industry. He redefined the rules of success, crashing meetings with all three major sports leagues without an invitation and getting hired for (and occasionally fired from) high-profile jobs for which he wasn't yet qualified. Despite his setbacks, he managed to avoid any loss of confidence or enthusiasm, and his glass half-full attitude, coupled with his unrelenting perseverance, made it possible for him to help invent and define what has become a multi-billion industry.

In his own words, 'Everyone fails. There's nothing conclusive about failure, but not getting back up and trying again, *that's* conclusive. And when you do fail, it's best to fail fast and to always fail forward, being certain to integrate the lessons learned from the mistakes made at the last stop.'

To me, his level of self-confidence and self-proclaimed 'moxie' made him seem a different kind of human being from me, one possessed of qualities I was pretty sure would never be part of my world. But then a question occurred to me that brought everything he'd been saying into focus: 'On a scale from 0 percent to 100 percent, how much say do you think you have in how things turn out?'

Without hesitation, he answered, 'Fifty-one percent,' meaning that he felt that in any situation he had a better than even chance of prevailing. He went on to point out that he'd not only achieved everything he'd achieved with '51 percent certainty,' but that he'd bet on himself 10 times out of 10 with those odds.

While I've not done the math (and wouldn't necessarily believe it if I had), 51 percent odds of winning in life sounds about right to me. There are an incredible number of success factors that are largely or even completely outside our control, including the environment/culture we're working in, the behavior of other people in that environment/culture, our current skill level, the level of competition we're facing, and the 'fickle finger of fate.'

So, achieving results isn't completely down to us, even though we may believe it is. That belief tends to act as a deterrent to our own best efforts. If I believe success is completely up (or down) to me, I'll either become a control freak, a stressed-out overachiever, or both. If I believe it's nothing to do with me, I'll probably do the minimum necessary to keep my job and my head above water, feeling lucky when things do go my way and disconnected from the people around me and the tasks at hand.

But 51 percent is different. It doesn't guarantee you anything, but it does:

- give you control of the board of a company

- get you kicked out of every casino in the world

- give you a reason to show up fully without putting any pressure on yourself to succeed

It allows you to invest fully in the direction you are heading without undue investment in the details. It directs you away from plans, schemes, and timetables and toward opportunities to get in the game and excel. Knowing that the path is almost always unpredictable and uncontrollable but that you have a say in how things turn out takes the pressure off you to predict and control the future and leaves your attention firmly in the here and now.

One final thought: when I brought the 51 percent idea up as part of a leadership keynote presentation, someone in the audience asked if it was similar to 'flying by the seat of your pants.' After a moment of reflection, I responded, 'It's like flying by the seat of your pants with one addition – the realization that your pants are made to fly!'

How did you show up to your impossible project today?

What did you do? What did you notice? What happened?

DAY 37

Snakes, Ladders, and Success

'Time is a game played beautifully by children.'
HERMANN HESSE

Imagine your impossible project being square 100 on a 'Snakes and Ladders' (in America 'Chutes and Ladders') board. Each time it's your turn, you roll the dice and move forward the allotted number of spaces, heading toward it.

At first it seems as though there should be some kind of mathematical formula for calculating how long it will take to get there. But it's not a linear process. Some turns, you land on a ladder and it shoots you forward 10 spaces; other turns, you land on a snake (or chute) and it sets you back five.

This means that sometimes you will get where you're headed much quicker than you were expecting; at other times it will seem to take forever and you may despair of ever arriving.

Of course, anything's possible, including not getting to the target if the dice of life don't roll your way, but the game is actually rigged in your favor. There are more ladders than snakes, so over time the odds are that you'll reach square 100 if you simply stay in the game long enough.

What if it were really that simple?

As you move forward with your impossible project, if there's something you want to do, have, or achieve, you're free to go about doing, having, or achieving it. Simply 'roll the dice' with each conversation you have or action you take, knowing that the pre-existing layout of the board takes care of the rest.

Sometimes, you won't get where you're headed. Surprisingly often, you will. The journey is nearly always as interesting as the destination, and the destination is nearly always nothing like you expected.

How did you show up to your impossible project today?

What did you do? What did you notice? What happened?

DAY 38

Getting in over Your Head

'Ever since I was a child I have had this instinctive urge for expansion and growth. To me, the function and duty of a quality human being is the sincere and honest development of one's potential.'

BRUCE LEE

The first time I gave a professional presentation back in 1990, I mapped it out in 30 to 90-second increments and created a full-page three-column outline complete with time stamps so I could tell if I was running behind schedule. On the plus side, I felt relatively relaxed that I would get through the talk in one piece; on the minus side, there was no real room for anything fresh or creative to come through me.

When I finally saw this, I decided to conduct an experiment. For a full year, I deliberately didn't prepare for anything in advance. I didn't plan out any talks, workshops, or even multi-day trainings. I didn't think through what I might say or focus on before sales calls or coaching sessions; I just showed up and responded to what showed up.

Now the truth is that not everything I did that year was great, and there were times when I wished I'd prepared a bit more than I did. But what I learned beyond a shadow of a doubt was that I really *could* trust the invisible giant of the creative mind to come through me and to guide me if I put myself in situations where I had to rely on it.

When you're a little kid and you genuinely don't understand the concept of traffic, it makes a certain kind of sense for your parents to scare you into not crossing the street. But you don't need the inner pressure of fear to keep you safe. Once you understand how traffic works, you have everything you need.

Similarly, once you understand that you have the potential to far exceed what you think are your limits, the capacity to solve problems that look unsolvable, and the ability to reach goals that look unreachable, you don't need that pressure anymore. You don't need to be pushed off the cliff anymore. You jump, because you recognize that it's only once we jump that we abandon our personal thinking in favor of the wider resource of Mind.

There's a poem I've always loved by Guillaume Apollinaire that speaks to this point:

> *'Come to the cliff,' he said.*
> *They said, 'We are afraid.'*
> *'Come to the cliff,' he said.*
> *They came. He pushed them. And they flew.*

Today, find as many opportunities as you can to get in over your head. Put yourself into at least one situation where you are unprepared and don't know how things are going to turn out. Just show up and respond to what happens.

You're either going to get self-conscious, flounder a bit, and muddle through, or you're going to get self-conscious, flounder a bit, find your feet, and begin to thrive.

How did you show up to your impossible project today?

What did you do? What did you notice? What happened?

DAY 39

Innate Wisdom

*'Don't let the noise of others' opinions
drown out your own inner voice.'*
STEVE JOBS

Let me take you through some highlights from a typical day in my life, first as I have experienced them in the past and then again as I see them today:

Up at 6:30 a.m. *Shake off the sweetness of sleep, grab my phone from the bedside table, and head to the bathroom for my morning routine. Have a debate with the gremlin in my head about whether or not to check my email – the gremlin wins, as per usual. After quickly reading through the headlines of the day ahead, it occurs to me to put the phone down and read the quiet of my mind. Refreshed and inspired, I make a mental note to argue harder against the gremlin tomorrow morning.*

At my desk at 10 a.m., *having finished my second or third coaching call/ webinar/interview of the day. Am about to check Facebook when it occurs to me I haven't yet seen my wife. Pop upstairs and make a coffee as we chat around the kitchen island. We laugh and connect over the puppies and kittens and politics of her Facebook feed, and when I return to my office half an hour later I feel grounded and reconnected to what matters most. I write in my notebook: 'Be sure to spend quality time with Nina every day!'*

Lunchtime, *and feeling a bit frazzled, I make myself an omelette and debate whether to eat it in front of a recent episode of a detective series, today's* SportsCenter *highlights, this week's* The Week, *or one of the new business books piling up on my desk. I settle on the detective show, but around 20 minutes in*

I get sleepy and close my eyes. Half an hour later I wake up refreshed, clear-headed, and head back downstairs to work on a chapter for the new book. Before I get stuck in, I make another notebook entry along the lines of: 'I'm never more than one nap away from a whole new experience of being alive.'

5:30 p.m. and feeling done for the day. The gremlin and I have another debate, this time about whether I have a drink and begin my evening routine or go workout. Today, working out wins. I feel that heady combination of endorphins from the workout, pride from winning the daily private victory over sloth, and guilt over feeling so proud of myself for essentially moving my legs up and down very quickly in a darkened room full of sweaty office workers.

Am I working out to feed my ego? I wonder. Should I not do it unless I'm really inspired to? Or do I need to double down and create an accountability system to make sure I work out every evening lest I become an out-of-shape overweight alcoholic?

As I head back to my car, I realize I'm overthinking things (again) and laugh out loud at my own craziness. On the drive home, I let myself bathe in the bubbliness of my endorphins without the contamination of my habitual thinking and make a mental note to write down 'Don't think so much' in my notebook when I get home.

Bedtime. Nina and I drift off watching an episode of Poldark and as I close my eyes a Syd Banks quote about dropping ego comes to mind. The last thought I remember thinking is that I really must find the full quote and print it off to stick on my computer screen as a daily reminder...

Here's what my notebook looked like an hour into the next morning:

No email for the first hour of the day!

Be sure to spend quality time with Nina.

Take naps!

We're all fundamentally okay — we're just overthinking things.

'...what we have been learning to do, is dropping ego, in turn is dropping beliefs, in turn is dropping anger, in turn is dropping ignorance, in turn is dropping sickness, and so on and so forth. It's the absolute supreme secret to all problems in the universe.' (Syd Banks)

Wait a minute – what if I don't need to write all this stuff down? What if I'm getting real-time instruction from my own innate wisdom on how to stay on track and get back on track when I need to?

This could change everything – if I actually trusted that the intelligence that designed me knows how to live me. If I saw that I don't need to remember any of these things because the reminders are already built into the system.

When I needed to drop email and get quiet, I did. When it was a good time for me to hang out with Nina, it occurred to me to go hang out with Nina. When I was tired, I had a nap. When I was overthinking working out, my own consciousness woke me up to how much I was overthinking it. Even the Syd Banks quote came to mind at the perfect time for me.

My wisdom is already unfolding as if by design. There's nothing I need to remember or to do...

For today, I invite you to notice just how often just the right thing occurs to you at just the right time for it to occur.

What would it be like if you could rely on this to guide you? How much easier would your impossible project be if you didn't need to be in charge of keeping yourself on track from day to day and moment to moment?

How did you show up to your impossible project today?

What did you do? What did you notice? What happened?

DAY 40

God Winks

'Coincidences are spiritual puns.'

G.K. CHESTERTON

One day I was walking through a bookstore, looking for something to spark some insight into a challenge I was facing with a client. Before I could get to the business section, I brushed against one of the shelves and a book literally fell on my head. When I picked it up off the floor, I saw that the title was *God Winks: A Guide to Coincidence in our Lives.*

I'm somewhat embarrassed to admit that at first I put the book back on the shelf and started to walk away, but in the end it seemed like too much of a coincidence to ignore. I went back, opened it up to a random page, and sure enough, there was the perfect answer to my question.

While not all synchronicities are that dramatic, most of us have had the sense of certain parts of our life having been guided – times when all we had to do was listen to the whispers and the next step almost magically appeared.

While it's certainly possible to read too much into such coincidences, in my experience it's equally possible to overlook them entirely. As Carl Jung said, 'Synchronicity is an ever-present reality for those who have eyes to see.'

Today, make a note of any coincidences, synchronicities, or seemingly chance meetings that have already come your way as you've been working on your impossible project.

How differently would you approach things if you knew that you could rely on 'Providence moving too'?

Because if there's one thing I've learned in over 25 years of shepherding dreams into reality, it's that aiming yourself in the direction of your dreams and taking the next step is all you need to do to travel further than you can imagine.

How did you show up to your impossible project today?

What did you do? What did you notice? What happened?

DAY 41

Let Go and Let...

'I can find only three kinds of business in the universe: mine, yours, and God's... Anything that's out of my control, your control, and everyone else's control – I call that God's business.'

BYRON KATIE

I had a conversation years ago with a religious leader who pointed out that in rejecting religion for rational reasons, the baby of a higher power often gets thrown out with the bathwater of historical beliefs and behavioral restrictions.

I was reminded of this when I walked into a local coffee shop and saw this written up on a chalk board behind the counter:

> GOOD MORNING, THIS IS GOD.
> I WILL BE HANDLING ALL YOUR
> PROBLEMS TODAY.
> I WON'T BE NEEDING YOUR HELP,
> SO HAVE A GREAT DAY!

Despite the fact that I haven't been religious since childhood, there was something about that I found incredibly comforting.

What if you really could just show up and leave anything that wasn't right in front of you to the creative intelligence within you?

What if you didn't have to handle the stuff that you didn't know how to handle, didn't have to make things happen that you didn't know how to make happen, and didn't have to do what you didn't know how to do?

Why, if that were true, you could just let go and let whatever it is that makes things happen do what it does best…

That is, for me, the real meaning behind the phrase 'let go and let God.' Not that we are meant to give up on our hopes and dreams, but that when we give up on thinking that we're in charge of the universe, whatever force that spins the planets and illuminates the stars can move heaven and Earth to make the seemingly impossible possible.

How did you show up to your impossible project today?

What did you do? What did you notice? What happened?

DAY 42

Rest, Review, Recharge, and Renew

'Make the most of yourself by fanning the tiny inner sparks of possibility into flames of achievement.'

GOLDA MEIR

The Week in Review

- I put in the hours on my project:

  ☐   ☐

  Yes   No

- I took my hands off the wheel of my project and noticed what showed up:

  ☐   ☐   ☐   ☐

  Not at all   Rarely   Sometimes   Daily

  What I did:

  ....

  ....

  ....

  ....

What I noticed:

. . . .

. . . .

. . . .

. . . .

What happened:

. . . .

. . . .

. . . .

. . . .

WEEK 7

MEASURING PROGRESS

'There are two possible outcomes: if the result confirms the hypothesis, then you've made a measurement. If the result is contrary to the hypothesis, then you've made a discovery.'

ENRICO FERMI

Michel Lotito, also known as 'Monsieur Mangetout,' ate approximately nine tons of metal during his lifetime, including multiple bicycles, chandeliers, television sets, and over one two-year period, an entire airplane. What makes that even more incredible is that he averaged only one kilogram a day. He is, to my mind, the ultimate example of someone who understands the principle of breaking down a task into 'bite-sized chunks.'

When we're working in the realm of linear projects and goals, progress is easy enough to track. We *can* break down the project into bite-sized chunks (perhaps not quite so literally as Monsieur Mangetout) and track the number of chunks we've been able to get through in the time allotted.

But what if our project doesn't lend itself to that kind of tracking? What if the results won't be apparent until we're getting close to the finish line?

This week, we'll explore both types of measures – the external, visible ones that vary from project to project and the internal ones that are harder to see but more universal in nature…

IMPOSSIBLE CHALLENGE NO.7: 'DONE' LISTS

This week, your impossible challenge is to keep a 'done' list – a list of everything you have actually done in support of your impossible project. This is the opposite of a 'to do' list – you add things to it throughout the day instead of crossing them off. By the end of the week, you'll have a clear sense of how much (or how little) you've actually been doing to create your project and how much (or how little) it's visibly contributed to the bottom-line result!

DAY 43

KPI vs UPI

'I have been struck again and again by how important measurement is to improving the human condition.'

BILL GATES

As a part of my own quest for a more non-linear approach to productivity, I joined a CEO group a couple of years ago. During our first session, everyone was talking about their 'KPIs,' or Key Performance Indicators.

As a general rule, KPIs have certain things in common. The first is that they are 'objective and observable,' meaning they track either behavior, results, or both, things like:

- 'How many sales calls are my team making?'

- 'How many new client contacts are they getting?'

- 'What's our weekly/monthly/quarterly revenue to budget?'

- 'What's our trailing revenue for the last 12 months?'

The second thing they all have in common is they don't have much in common – they're individualized to each business or project.

For example, here are some KPIs I've seen people apply to an impossible project of losing 60 pounds in 90 days. (Please note, I'm not suggesting any of these are 'good or bad' – they're just examples!)

- Losing 5 pounds a week or 1 pound a day.

- Eating 1,200 calories or less than 20g of carbohydrates a day.

- Walking at least 10,000 steps a day.

- Going down one pants size per week.

The holy grail amongst KPIs is finding 'leading indicators,' which are predictive and let us know how things are going long before the results start to show up on the outside, allowing the business to self-correct and adapt to changing circumstances.

I wrestled for about six months to find useful data to track in my own business before I had an epiphany: the most reliable leading indicators in my business were almost 180 degrees away from traditional KPIs – internally measured and subjective (though still observable). Better still, they were highly predictive, even in highly volatile endeavors. I called them 'Universal Performance Indicators' (UPIs), because they turned out to be universal – relevant across the board for pretty much anyone for pretty much anything.

Over the course of this week, I'll be sharing some of the most useful Universal Performance Indicators I've seen in my work with individuals and companies.

 In the meantime, take some time today to explore these questions for yourself:

- What are some KPIs for your impossible project? In other words, what are the results, actions, time-frames, or other external indicators that might consistently predict how well your project is progressing?

- What are some UPIs for your impossible project? In other words, what are the internal factors that might consistently predict how well your project is progressing?

How did you show up to your impossible project today?

What did you do? What did you notice? What happened?

DAY 44

Why Optimism and Pessimism Get in the Way of Measurement

'Not everything that can be measured is important, and not everything that is important can be measured.'

ALBERT EINSTEIN

One of my coaches once described my business strategy as being 'like a man whose job it is to lay railroad tracks.' He pointed out that I was always running just ahead of the train, laying tracks as fast as I could in fear that if I didn't, the train would derail. Every now and again I'd get far enough ahead to take a break, but then I'd hear that whistle blowing and the whole process would begin again.

When we dug deeper into that analogy, it became clear to me that I was using my feelings of optimism or pessimism as a primary indicator of how things were going. If I felt that they were going badly, I'd work as hard as I could to turn them around; if I felt that they were going well, I'd let the status quo carry on and turn my attention to relaxing and enjoying my life.

The problem with this strategy (besides the constant stress and exhaustion it engendered in me) was that it was based on a fundamental misunderstanding of how the mind worked.

It looks as though our feelings of optimism and pessimism are a reflection of how things are going and a predictor of future performance, but all they actually tell us about is our current thinking. In other words:

Our feelings are only and always a perfect barometer of the flow and content of the energy of Thought in the moment.

165

Because I didn't understand that, when my thinking was mostly made up of positive imaginings about future success, I felt optimistic about the future and assumed everything was going well. When my thoughts were mostly made up of dark imaginings about pointless efforts and inevitable failure, I'd feel pessimistic about the future and assume everything was going badly.

What has been interesting is seeing how much easier it is to work on a project once how it's going is divorced from how I'm feeling about it. It frees me up to experience all the ups and downs of my emotional life while continuing to move forward with my goals and projects.

- What thoughts and insights does this distinction prompt in you?

- How would your own approach to and experience of your impossible project be different if optimism was no better than pessimism as a performance measure?

- What inner measures (UPIs) might still prove useful?

How did you show up to your impossible project today?

What did you do? What did you notice? What happened?

DAY 45

UPI No.1: Are You Inspired?

'What the world needs is people who have come alive.'

HOWARD THURMAN

Have you ever been so inspired by a subject that you stayed up late studying it? Have you ever got so into a project that you had to make yourself (or be told to) stop working on it and go back to your 'real job,' or even stop to eat?

While inspiration is often equated with enthusiasm, it's a closer cousin to fascination – a genuine interest in a particular topic or goal.

While it may seem as though it's the result of something outside us, it's actually a capacity *inside* us. We'll naturally become fascinated with pretty much anything to which we give our full attention. It's built into our system. And that fascination will in turn heighten our senses, allow us to respond intelligently and directly to the world around us, and bring forth fresh thought from the invisible giant of our creative mind.

Allowing yourself to become inspired by your impossible project will lead you to higher levels of engagement and resilience. You won't have to remind yourself to make time to work on your project, though you may have to remind yourself to take time for other things.

Time and energy will even become more malleable. You might feel exhausted one moment and then your imagination will catch fire and you'll think, *Well, maybe I could make one more call! Well, maybe I could put in just one more hour! Well, maybe I could paint one more bit of this! Well, maybe I could talk to one more person!*

And because you're inspired, it won't even matter so much how things are going. You'll be more interested in the project than the result. You'll tend to get fresh new ideas and insights without even having to go and look for them. You'll start to notice new possibilities and opportunities on a regular basis. And if you keep seeing new possibilities, some of them will inevitably come to fruition.

That's not to say your mood won't go up and down. Thought will still be a constant variable. But as long as you allow yourself to be really present and engaged with your impossible project, you'll be able to ride out your moods and keep moving forward with your creation.

Your homework today is to check out how inspired you are by your project.

If your level of inspiration is high, you'll get fresh ideas and insights that will help you create results beyond the linear cause and effect of putting in the hours.

If it's low, take a few steps back and notice what you notice. Have you begun to lose heart and believe it will never happen? Have you started to think *If it's to be, it's up to me* and exhausted yourself with thinking about how much work it's going to take?

Reconnect with your inspiration – not by 'faking it,' but by asking yourself these questions:

● 'What was the inspiration that originally led me to begin this project?'

● 'What fascinates me about this project, or could fascinate me if I let it?'

● 'What am I most curious about?'

● 'How much fun could I have working on this?'

How did you show up to your impossible project today?

What did you do? What did you notice? What happened?

DAY 46

UPI No.2: Are You Engaged?

'Our repeated failure to fully act as we would wish must not discourage us. It is the sincere intention that is the essential thing, and this will in time release us from the bondage of habits which at present seem almost insurmountable.'

THOMAS TROWARD

There's a story I share in my book Supercoach *about a four-star general who was taking a tour of a company that had been hired to complete a major defense contract.*

Despite the CEO's assurance that this particular project would be completed on time, the general felt that the team was not 100 percent committed to getting the job done. He argued that they should remain at work and do whatever it took to succeed, even if it meant working much longer hours, taking extra time away from home and family, and putting themselves under additional personal pressure and stress. He told the CEO that understanding personnel management was like eating bacon and eggs for breakfast: the chicken was 'involved,' but the pig was 'committed.'

The contractor smiled and said, 'Well, that's true, general, but the pig is dead and the chicken is still producing eggs. I want my people to stay "involved."'

The general backed down and the project was completed on time.

While I'm not sure that encounter ever actually happened, it's clear that our level of involvement in an outcome plays a huge part in whether or not that outcome is achieved.

I tend to use the word 'engagement' to describe being involved and committed, but you could use any word that points to our capacity to go 'all in' on any project as opposed to creeping around the margins. As a TV director once pointed out to me, 'Nobody wants to watch tentative acting any more than they want to have tentative sex.'

We could also use the word 'resolve,' in the sense that when a question is resolved, it's off the table and no longer on our mind. And when whether or not we're going to move forward with our impossible dream is no longer on the table, our mind is free and available to take advantage of the 'whole stream of events' that issues forth when we show up and aim ourselves in a clear direction.

Simply put, if we've got a high level of engagement, it won't particularly matter how our project seems to be going at any given moment. We're going to stay in the game because we really want to be in the game.

For today, take a look at your level of engagement with your impossible project.

Know that if your level is high, chances are that good results will follow in time.

If your level is low, success is still possible — you're just more likely to take yourself out of the game when things aren't going your way.

To boost your level of engagement, you need only pay attention to two factors:

● Are you clear about what you're up to? (intention)

● Are you actively in the game? (involvement)

How did you show up to your impossible project today?

What did you do? What did you notice? What happened?

DAY 47

UPI No.3: Are You Taking Things a Little Bit Too Seriously?

'Angels fly because they take themselves lightly.'

G.K. CHESTERTON

Many years ago I had a very serious client who asked me (in all seriousness) whether or not I thought he was serious enough. I laughed, but he didn't, so I asked him why he wanted to be seen as serious. His answer, which I thought was kind of funny, was because it would help him be taken more seriously.

I pointed out to him that competence and seriousness were unrelated. Then I shared a story with him that I originally read in a book called *The Art of Possibility* by the gifted conductor Benjamin Zander and his wife, Rosamund:

> *Two prime ministers are sitting in a room discussing affairs of state. Suddenly a man bursts in, apoplectic with fury, shouting and stamping and banging his fist on the table.*
>
> *The resident prime minister admonishes him. 'Peter,' he says, 'kindly remember rule number six.'*
>
> *Peter is instantly restored to complete calm. He apologizes and withdraws.*
>
> *The politicians return to the conversation, only to be interrupted 20 minutes later by a hysterical woman, hair flying, gesticulating wildly.*
>
> *The intruder is greeted with the words: 'Marie, please remember rule number six.'*

Complete calm descends once more, and she too withdraws with a bow and an apology.

When the scene is repeated for a third time, the visiting prime minister addresses his colleague: 'My dear friend, I've seen many things in my life but never anything as remarkable as this. Would you be willing to share with me the secret of rule number six?'

'Very simple,' replies the resident prime minister. 'Rule number six is: "Don't take yourself so goddamned seriously."'

'Ah,' says his visitor, 'that is a fine rule.' After a moment of pondering, he enquires, 'And what, may I ask, are the other rules?'

'There aren't any.'

One of the things that can happen when we start to measure progress is that creating the impossible stops feeling like a game and starts feeling like a responsibility. We start to add weight and meaning to success or failure, and dilute our present-moment wisdom with historical insecurity. In short, we start to make evaluating progress more important than the possibility of creation.

In fact, the lack of lightheartedness that taking ourselves too seriously engenders actually impedes our creativity and will. It flattens our natural buoyancy and enthusiasm, and makes everything we do that little bit harder and that little bit heavier.

Syd Banks once said, 'Of course you've got to make a profit for your business; that's common sense. But if you don't take it seriously and do the same things, you'll make the same money. As a matter of fact, it's far, far better because you're having a good time doing it.'

And when we're enjoying the process, we tend to show up more willingly and our entire project becomes infused with joy.

On a scale from 1 to 10, how 'heavy' or 'light' does your impossible project feel? How would that number shift if you remembered that:

- Enjoyment and engagement tend to go hand in hand. In other words, it's easy to engage with what you enjoy doing, and the more engaged you are with what you're doing, the more you tend to enjoy it (Chapter 4).

- You're no better off as a human being when you win than when you lose (Day 24).

- Making progress is only 51 percent up to you, but 51 percent is more than enough (Day 36).

How did you show up to your impossible project today?

What did you do? What did you notice? What happened?

DAY 48

Making It Real

'When you can measure what you are speaking about, and express it in numbers, you know something about it; but when you cannot measure it, when you cannot express it in numbers, your knowledge is of a meager and unsatisfactory kind; it may be the beginning of knowledge, but you have scarcely in your thoughts advanced to the stage of science.'

SIR WILLIAM THOMSON, LORD KELVIN

I've experimented with multiple project management tools over the years, but the ones that have worked best have inevitably been the ones I've either invented myself or adapted to specifically address my own unique working style.

In my business these days we tend to use a combination of KPIs and UPIs to track prospect calls and meetings, but are also making sure that our levels of inspiration, engagement and lightheartedness are at an eight-plus (on a scale of 10) across the board. If we can't get there, we either won't take on a project or we'll outsource it to someone who can.

How does this relate to your impossible project? Ultimately, the question you want to be able to answer is simply this:

'Am I on track or off-track to complete my impossible project in the time I've given myself to do so?'

For today, your assignment is simple: decide what measures of progress you will be tracking over the next six weeks and set up the simplest way of keeping track that occurs to you. You can use online tools, project management software, pen and paper, or the 'Rest, Review, Recharge, and Renew' pages of this book.

How did you show up to your impossible project today?

What did you do? What did you notice? What happened?

DAY 49

Rest, Review, Recharge, and Renew

*'You have capacities within you that are phenomenal,
if you only knew how to release them.'*

DAVID BOHM

The Week in Review

- I put in the hours on my project:

☐   ☐

Yes   No

- I kept a 'done' list showing everything I did in support of my project:

☐   ☐

Yes   No

What I did:

....

....

....

....

What I noticed:

....

....

....

....

What happened:

....

....

....

....

CREATING IN A WORLD OF THOUGHT

'Having no unusual coincidence is far more unusual than any coincidence could possibly be.'

ISAAC ASIMOV

By now, you've probably got a pretty good sense of what you're aiming at and you're showing up to your impossible project (and responding to what shows up) on a regular basis.

So this is a good time to take a deeper look at the nature of Thought. We'll examine how seeing the natural fluidity of our thinking impacts the way we respond to problems and handle time, money, productivity, and the unknown...

IMPOSSIBLE CHALLENGE NO.8: THE WHEELBARROW TEST

Your challenge this week is to take a fresh look at anything in your life that can't be placed in a wheelbarrow. Why? Throughout this book I'm asserting that 100 percent of our experience is made of Thought. By definition, anything that doesn't pass the wheelbarrow test can only exist in Thought, so your experience of it is subject to change when you get insightful new thinking!

179

DAY 50

Why We Do What We Do
(and Don't Do What We Don't)

'How people perform correlates to how
situations occur to them.'

STEVE ZAFFRON AND DAVE LOGAN

There is one universal 'cause' of all human behavior:

We do what we do because it seems like a good idea at the time in our thought-created inner world.

We're always making the best choices we can, given the way the world looks to us at the time. And the way the world looks to us is 100 percent a product of thought.

We instinctively know this, which is why, when and if we regret our actions later, our first words are inevitably 'What was I thinking?'

The principle of Thought accounts for why something can seem an obviously good idea one moment and an obviously bad one in the next. It's what allows us to see infinite possibilities for the future or convince ourselves there's only one possibility and it's decidedly not the one we want to happen. Thought turns molehills into mountains, and inspiration into invention. It is the 'play dough' of the universe, endlessly being shaped and re-shaped into the realities we live in.

To the extent that we see the thought-created nature of our personal reality, we are free to think anything, feel anything, and do anything in any situation. Contrary to many people's fears, this does not lead to a more chaotic life. Rather, it makes space for our deeper mind – the intelligence behind the system – to guide us through the maze of human experience with grace, creativity and wisdom.

Understanding how Thought works takes a lot of the fear and superstition out of life. In the same way that we can take a lot of the fear out of watching a scary movie by looking away from the screen toward the projector, when we look away from our experience toward what is creating our experience – the principle of Thought in action – much of our fear begins to evaporate.

When we see just how much of what we think of as life is created via our own thinking, it settles us down and makes us more reflective. We take the foot off the gasoline of our habitual thinking and begin to experience new insights. We connect more deeply with others because we're not so preoccupied with our thinking about ourselves. We live more in the creative flow of inspiration and move more quickly through problems and challenges.

And that in turn makes it easier for us to create what we really want to create, even though from time to time it looks impossible in our mind.

Take some time today to contemplate this quote from Syd Banks:

'Every human being is doing the best they can,
given the thinking they have that looks real to them.'

If this were 100 percent true, what would that mean for you in the creation of your impossible project?

How did you show up to your impossible project today?

What did you do? What did you notice? What happened?

DAY 51

Like a Rat in a Maze

*'The trouble with being in the rat race is that
even if you win, you're still a rat.'*

LILY TOMLIN

Some of the most invisible products of the principle of Thought are the 'givens' we attempt to navigate in our lives. For example, one of the most frequently asked questions people ask me as we move past the halfway point in this program is some variation on 'How on earth can I complete my impossible project in the next six weeks?'

If that were all there was to the question, the creative force inside each one of us would instantly go to work providing so many answers that our only problem would be choosing our favorites from the menu. But the unspoken 'givens' make things a bit more complicated than that.

'Given that...

- I'm not very good with people,

- The economy is terrible,

- I've no evidence that I can do it and plenty of evidence that I can't,

- I wouldn't want anyone to think I'm being pushy,

- It's probably already too late,

- I'm being selfish to even consider taking money out of other people's pockets,

- If I was more spiritual, I wouldn't even care about this,

...how can I complete my impossible project in the next six weeks?'

Notice the difference?

So, what can we do about this hidden maze of self-defeating thoughts?

Imagine you are a rat in a maze. You know there's a lump of cheese waiting for you somewhere, and that the only way to get it is to run the maze successfully and faster than any of the other rats. So you put all your resources into learning strategies of successful maze running and developing your stamina and speed.

Over time you begin to experience more and more success, and although it's wearing you down and negatively impacting your relationships, your slowly growing pile of cheddar fuels a commitment to learning even more strategies and training even harder.

Until ... one day you wake up and realize that you're only imagining that you're a rat in a maze. From that moment forward, you're once again free to tap into the infinite creative potential of the deeper mind and put your wisdom to work in the simple, uncontaminated pursuit of a simple, uncontaminated objective. No maze necessary.

The minute we recognize that we're stuck in a maze of our own creation, the creative intelligence behind the mind will think for us. It will re-create our situation, our apparent circumstances, so that they don't seem so problematic.

In other words, the way out of the rat race isn't to get better at racing. It's to allow the system to reset and the creative intelligence behind the mind to take us back to the drawing board. After all, anything is possible and everything is up for grabs — right up until the moment that you once again decide that it isn't.

How did you show up to your impossible project today?

What did you do? What did you notice? What happened?

DAY 52

Bending Time

'An hour sitting with a pretty girl on a park bench passes like a minute, but a minute sitting on a hot stove seems like an hour.'

ALBERT EINSTEIN, ON RELATIVITY

There's an old joke about a very clever man who somehow manages to get himself up to heaven on a day pass and sits down to have a conversation with God.

He asks, 'God, can you explain how eternity looks to you?'

God replies, 'To me, all of eternity is like a blink of an eye – less than one second in your limited perception of time.'

Next the man asks, 'God, can you explain what wealth is like for you?'

And God says, 'Wealth is so much more infinite than you can imagine. A billion dollars in the infinite realm is like a penny in your limited perception of wealth.'

The man thinks for a moment.

'God – can I borrow a penny?'

'Sure,' says God. 'Just a second...'

Nearly all time-management systems are based on the idea that time is a fixed quantity. But you can't put time in a wheelbarrow, which means that it is less subject to the laws of physics than it is to the principles of Mind, Thought, and Consciousness.

In other words, time is a concept we've made up to help ourselves coordinate action and make sense of things in the world. And since it's made up, our experience of it is 100 percent an experience of Thought. What if, instead of learning to manage linear time, we could learn to 'bend it' – to take advantage of our capacity to think differently and have a different experience?

What happens when time bends?

1. Life becomes more black and white

One of the reasons deadlines work for the people they work for is that when we take a deadline to heart, we organize our priorities and focus on what we need to do. The answer to questions becomes 'yes,' 'no,' or 'I can't think about that right now.' Getting it done can become more important than how well it gets done. But it gets done.

2. We're less inclined to indulge our thinking

Not long after we moved to America, I sat down to prepare a log of how much time I was spending on all my work projects so that I could persuade my wife I really didn't have 'extra time' to help out with the house and kids. To my dismay, I found I was spending less than two hours a day actually working and 10 to 12 hours thinking about what there was to be done.

I never did show my wife my time log, but I did start volunteering to help out with a lot more tasks around the house. And as soon as I had less time or inclination to overthink everything, I started to get considerably more done in considerably less time.

3. We let the small stuff take care of itself along the way

A professor places a large jar on the table. Beside it she places a bucket of gravel, a bucket of sand, a bucket of water, and three big rocks. She then challenges his class to find a way to fit everything into the jar.

After numerous attempts, it becomes clear that the only way to do it is to start with the big rocks first. Then the gravel fills the space between the big rocks, the sand fills the gaps in the gravel, and the water fills the gaps between the sand.

When we put our attention on the big rocks in our impossible project and don't let ourselves get caught up in the daily gravel, ground down by the sand, or swept away by the water, it's amazing how much of what we thought we had to do 'just happens' while we're busy showing up to what matters most.

Here are some questions that will give you the experience of time being less fixed and more fluid going forward:

- What's the longest hour you've ever spent? How about the shortest day or week? Why?

- The next time you have a deadline, notice what happens to your thinking. Does it get easier or harder to ignore? What do you make of that?

- Is your impossible project one of your biggest 'rocks' right now? What are the one, two, or three things you would focus on if you knew the rest of your life would fit itself in around them?

How did you show up to your impossible project today?

What did you do? What did you notice? What happened?

DAY 53

The Value of Money

'Price is what you pay. Value is what you get.'
WARREN BUFFET

I don't know what the first official financial transaction was, but I love the idea that it might have involved two neighboring farmers trading several chickens for a milking goat. No doubt there were grumblings from both sides of the fence, and while both sides now had access to eggs and milk, they both felt slightly ripped off in the exchange.

While for the most part we've moved beyond exchanging chickens for goats, the value of money has always been a moving target. It depends entirely on what you're trying to use the money for.

If you want to buy stuff, I highly recommend money. It's great for it. You can use it pretty much anywhere in the world to facilitate the exchange of goods and services. You don't even need to carry chickens and goats around with you anymore – you can make your way instead with bits of paper, plastic, and/or a decent internet connection.

But if you want to feel happy, confident, safe, and secure, money is a terrible tool for that job. It's completely unreliable because feelings are made of Thought. Since Thought is a transient energy, our feelings will always come and go with our thinking.

The reason money can seem like such a problem to us isn't just because we're trying to use it for something it has no power to impact. It's also because we have so much ossified thinking about it that we're rarely at our most creative or inspired when we're looking to get access to more of it.

Try this exercise to begin opening your mind around money today. You can do it in writing, or out loud with a friend, or even your favorite pet:

● Set a timer for 10 minutes.

● As soon as the timer starts, begin writing or sharing ideas for how you could access/make/have more money to use for your impossible project and/or generally in your life.

Here's the only rule: you're not allowed to write or talk about the economy, your past history with money, what you hope more money will do for you, why it's difficult for you, or anything other than:

'How can I access/make/have more money to use for my impossible project and/or generally in my life?'

Repeat as needed.

How did you show up to your impossible project today?

What did you do? What did you notice? What happened?

DAY 54

A Hybrid Model for Effortless Productivity

'Life begets life; energy creates energy. It is by spending oneself that one becomes rich.'
Sarah Bernhardt

When I got an early-model Prius hybrid back in 2004, I spent a remarkable amount of my driving time with one eye glued to the bit of the dashboard where you could see how much of your energy expenditure was coming from the electric engine and how much was coming from the gas engine. I soon learned that attempting to accelerate too quickly shifted it over into the gas zone, whereas easing up on the pedal a bit let the natural momentum of the car take over and the electric engine come back into play. Over time I got a feel for it, and I took a perverse delight in watching how many more miles to the gallon I was getting than my wife's gas-only turbocharged SUV.

I also came to see that learning to get the most out of driving a hybrid was a pretty good metaphor for learning to get more juice to the squeeze in everything you do. It's something like this (but not this).

We can accomplish remarkable things running on a blend of two different kinds of fuel:

- *Motivation* (i.e. willpower) works like gas in an internal combustion engine. It burns fast and strong, but runs out quickly and needs continual renewal. It also can take a toll on the engine itself. It's made up of a lot of personal thinking — the sum total of all of our ideas about who we are, what we're up to, why we're up to it (our 'motive'), and what we think we need to be doing to get where we want to be.

- *Inspiration* (let's call it 'spirit-power') works like the electric engine in a hybrid. It's a clean, non-toxic energy source which is self-renewing as it goes. It's still made up of thought, but it's more impersonal thought that seems to come from a deeper part of the mind. Inspiration comes to us and through us, and as a rule, it isn't about us, it's about whatever it is that we're working on or toward.

Imagine bringing your impossible dream to life is like driving a hybrid car to a seemingly distant destination. You start with a full charge of inspiration in your battery and a full reservoir of motivation in your gas tank.

If you pay no attention to which fuel you're burning when, chances are you'll use mostly gas, and the further you go, the more often you'll need to stop to fill back up. All that fuel can start to get expensive, and the wear and tear on the car requires you to spend even more time and energy keeping things maintained and fixing them when they break down.

If you try to only run on electricity, it can be difficult to get going, and you can become more obsessed with keeping your energy expenditure clean than actually getting where you set out to go.

A simple resolution comes the moment you realize that the car is designed to run on both gas and electricity — motivation and inspiration; willpower and spirit, personal and impersonal thinking. You never have to decide which energy source to use when — the system itself will effortlessly switch between them as needed.

Better still, as you get more of a feel for how the system is designed to work, you develop driving habits that optimize efficiency and effectiveness. When you're feeling stressed, wound up, or burned out, chances are you're running on a lot of personal thinking and not much inspiration. This is fine, as sometimes the car just needs a little extra gas to get where it's going. When you're feeling a sense of ease and flow, your electric engine is in full force with just enough personal will to keep things moving in the direction of your choosing.

This is an inexact metaphor, but the ideas behind it are simple:

- Thought is the fuel for all creation and achievement. Personal thinking (motivation) fuels the will; impersonal thinking (inspiration) fuels the spirit.

- You don't need to figure out which thoughts are the 'right' ones or when to use which kind – your mind is already designed to use an optimal balance of inspiration and motivation along the way.

How did you show up to your impossible project today?

What did you do? What did you notice? What happened?

DAY 55

Calling Forth the Creative Force

*'Man is always more than he can know of himself;
consequently, his accomplishments, time and
again, will come as a surprise to him.'*

HENRY WADSWORTH LONGFELLOW

Kaye Taylor is a serial entrepreneur who has founded and run multiple successful companies. Here's her story of creating the impossible in a world of Thought:

> *Before doing the 90-day program, I thought I was the one who was in control and that I could make things happen. And then in December 2014, I re-read Michael's* Inside-Out Revolution, *and it was like reading it for the first time. I just heard stuff in that book that I hadn't heard or seen before.*
>
> *So, my two colleagues, Dani and Steph, who had helped me launch a successful software company, and I all realized at around the same time that we were trying too hard with something that just wasn't flowing naturally, and we all agreed to just stop. And the 'Creating the Impossible' program came up and I thought,* Wow, it would be cool to do that.
>
> *I was in a very clear state of mind because I knew that it was right to stop what we had been doing. So even though it was very alien for me to be in the unknown, it actually felt very reassuring, as though I was in the right space.*
>
> *So we started that year in a bar in Edinburgh with nothing on our agenda and asked, 'What are we going to do?'*
>
> *And at one point I said, 'Wouldn't it be cool if we tried to set up a brand new business together?'*

And then, literally out of the blue, Dani said that she'd had a dream in which she'd seen some really beautiful slipper boots, and I just saw it. Something that I'm beginning to see more and more is that the more in tune I am with my own quiet voice of wisdom, the more I hear wisdom in others. And Steph heard it too, and we both said, 'That's what we're doing! Let's see if we can create some slipper boots and sell our first pair in 90 days, but with nothing on it.'

In a way, I think we were at an advantage because we genuinely knew nothing. We really had no experience to draw on. None of us knew how to draw, none of us knew anything about textile fabrics, none of us were designers, none of us had ever made anything tangible. But from a 'Creating the Impossible' perspective, this was perfect, because when you don't know, there's space for something new to come in.

But the next day I woke up thinking, What on Earth do I do now? *So I phoned up Edinburgh University and got through to a woman called Maria who was head of Product Design and Innovation. I admitted we knew nothing, and asked if she could point us in the right direction. She was curious about our project and met us. She said, 'Just start – just start making stuff now.'*

And we did. We probably made 150 prototypes. The first few were completely and utterly ridiculous. But now, a year later, we have a business called Innyoot.

Something that has really touched me deeply is how if you are open to anything, you experience opportunities that just wouldn't have come your way otherwise. I will give you a small example.

I went to the Philippines with my husband, who was on a business trip, and went into a fabric gallery that was run by a social entrepreneur who was supporting rural weaving communities. She happened to be there and I shared what we were up to. She was keen to get involved, but when we bought fabrics from her, they weren't stretchy enough.

I went back to her and said, 'Look, would one of the weaving communities be willing to experiment with some stretched thread?'

And just today she came back to me and said, 'I am so, so pleased that you challenged us to experiment, because we are now seeing that making this fabric opens up new doors for us.'

I was so touched, because it dawned on me that when you follow your heart and do something that you love, but aren't attached to a specific outcome, not only are you having the loveliest experience yourself, but you are impacting other people positively too. It is so different from how I experienced business in the past. It is much gentler and there is less expectation.

(To learn more about the Innyoot experience, visit www.innyoot.com!)

 Today's experiment is to reflect on how much space you are used to making for the creative force to come through you, and how things might be different with your impossible project if you allowed yourself to rely on that invisible giant even more...

How did you show up to your impossible project today?

What did you do? What did you notice? What happened?

DAY 56

Rest, Review, Recharge, and Renew

'Everything is impossible until it is done.'
ROBERT H. GODDARD

The Week in Review

- I put in the hours on my project:

☐   ☐

Yes   No

- I took a fresh look at anything in my life that couldn't be placed in a wheelbarrow:

☐   ☐   ☐   ☐

Not at all   Rarely   Sometimes   Daily

What I did:

. . . .

. . . .

. . . .

. . . .

What I noticed:

....

....

....

....

What happened:

....

....

....

....

WEEK 9

GETTING UNSTUCK

*'It is only when the mind refuses to flow with life, and
gets stuck at the banks, that it becomes a problem.'*

SRI NISARGADATTA MAHARAJ

When a stick gets stuck in a river, it doesn't need therapy, it needs a nudge back into the natural flow of water. Similarly, when we get stuck, we need a nudge back into the natural flow of creative thought.

This week, I'll be offering you a series of these 'nudges.' We'll be exploring creativity, problem-solving, hanging out in the unknown, and more...

IMPOSSIBLE CHALLENGE NO.9:
LETTING GO

This week your impossible challenge is to hold on to nothing. Let thoughts go as they arise. Get out of the way again and again and again and see what happens!

DAY 57

The Four Quadrants of Creation

'Creativity is not just for artists. It's for businesspeople looking for a new way to close a sale; it's for engineers trying to solve a problem; it's for parents who want their children to see the world in more than one way.'

TWYLA THARP

Think of a part of your impossible project you have thus far failed to achieve or create... Is that because you couldn't, you didn't really want to, or both?

This question speaks to the two primary components that lead to success in pretty much anything: commitment and competence.

- Commitment is our 'want to' – the amount of desire and willingness we bring to our project or creation.

- Competence is our 'how to' – the amount of skill and capability we are currently able to harness.

Here's a simple way of looking at how these two elements combine to create our experience of creating (or failing to create) what we want:

	Low Competence	High Competence
High Commitment	*The Learning Curve*	*Mastery*
Low Commitment	*The Great Unknown*	*Incidental Success*

Let's take a quick look at each of the four quadrants in turn:

I. Low commitment/low competence: the great unknown

Something we aren't particularly good at and don't particularly care about may seem to be irrelevant, and very often is. However, this quadrant can also be the gateway to a whole new experience.

What holds us back in life is rarely the problems we know about and are actively attempting to solve – it's what we don't know that we don't know. That doesn't mean we have to delve into everything in order to learn something, just that an active curiosity and a greater comfort with the unknown will serve us well, regardless of what we choose to do with our lifetime.

II. Low commitment/high competence: incidental success

I remember having a conversation with a friend once about what he was going to do 'when he grew up.' He said he would probably continue to work in the software industry, despite the fact that he didn't particularly like it. When I asked him why, he said, 'Because I'm good at it and it pays well.'

It's surprising how many of my clients have become successful at something they don't really care about; it's equally surprising how few of them have seriously considered basing their life and career decisions around what they would actually love to do. Once they do, they step onto...

III. High commitment/low competence: the learning curve

The larger the gap between our 'want to' and our skill set, the steeper the learning curve and the more we enjoy riding it. We oscillate between being overwhelmed and being in the pure flow as we learn what we need to learn in order to live the life we want to live.

Of course, if we don't recognize the need to develop the relevant skills or competencies, we're liable to fall off the curve altogether. But when we do put both elements together, we move into the final quadrant...

IV. High commitment/high competence: mastery

When our commitment and competency are both at their peak, we demonstrate mastery in our endeavors. It's not that things never go wrong or always work out, just that we are able to respond well to change and our best is often more than enough to create the results we want.

With mastery, things often look effortless, and can feel that way too. This isn't because there's no *actual* effort involved, rather that there's no 'effort*ing*' — no need to strive or struggle in order to succeed.

● To help understand each of these quadrants in relation to your impossible project, fill in the chart below (or create a larger version yourself) with a few activities and sub-goals related to your project:

	Low Competence	High Competence
High Commitment		
Low Commitment		

● Now, check in with the 'failure' you explored at the beginning of today's session, and if it's still relevant to your project, notice whether what's missing is really 'want to' or 'how to.'

If you're not sure that you 'want to,' check to see if this really is an essential part of your project or just something you think you need to do in order to create your desired end result. Authentic desire doesn't need to be created, simply uncovered, one limiting belief at a time, and given space to breathe and to grow.

● On the other hand, if all that's missing is the 'how to,' simply jump back onto the learning curve, practice what you need to practice, and enjoy the ride!

How did you show up to your impossible project today?

What did you do? What did you notice? What happened?

DAY 58

The Problem with Problem-Solving

'Problems are not the problem; coping is the problem.'
Virginia Satir

An entrepreneur was explaining to me his concerns about an upcoming meeting with a potential angel investor. He wanted tips on how to find the 'extra' confidence to make sure his pitch went 'really, really, *really* well.'

I told him that I could share tips with him, but what would make the biggest difference would be to have fun and not try to make this pitch any different from the ones that had led to this opportunity.

As I explained it to him, here's how 'the problem-solving cycle' usually works:

* Something happens.

  (In this case, he got the opportunity to meet with someone who might be able to help fund his company.)

* We imagine all the bad things – 'problems' – that might happen as a result of it.

  (In this case, what would happen if he suddenly lost his nerve in front of a potential investor and 'blew his big chance.')

* We then 'problem-solve' by doing things to prevent the bad things we've imagined from happening.

  (In this case, try to learn confidence techniques.)

The problem is, apart from the original event, nothing's actually happened except our over-reaction in the physical world to the problems in our imagination!

He didn't quite seem to get what I meant, so I told him the following story:

Imagine that you're the captain of a star cruiser and your spaceship is surrounded by hostile aliens. Your only hope is if the starfleet sends ships to come and save you.

A transmission comes through on your comms link. It's the starfleet commander.

He looks you straight in the eye and says, 'I've got some bad news and some good news... The bad news is that we're not sending any rescue ships. The good news is that you're not really in outer space and there aren't any aliens.'

The entrepreneur laughed, and called me a couple of days later to tell me the pitch had gone phenomenally well.

What can we learn from all this?

There will never be enough techniques to solve problems that don't actually exist.

Have fun, learn heaps, and relax — while life will always have its ups and downs, coping with them is inevitably much simpler than you think.

How did you show up to your impossible project today?

What did you do? What did you notice? What happened?

DAY 59

Have You Given Up Yet?

*'Some of us think holding on makes us strong,
but sometimes it is letting go.'*

HERMANN HESSE

One of my colleagues, Don Donovan, ran a large division of an international aerospace company that was given the impossible project of cutting production time on one of their military projects in half – from 18 months to nine months.

Alongside engineers from Cal Tech, MIT, Stanford, and the best schools in the country, they brainstormed ideas for weeks in the traditional way. They came up with one idea that would ultimately allow them to make the parts needed in the time allotted; unfortunately, it would take them at least a year to retool their factories to make the new process viable.

After about six weeks of intense exploration, Don called the team together and let them know he appreciated their efforts, but he was going to call the representatives from the military in the morning and let them know they wouldn't be able to complete the project on time, even though it would quite likely cost the company one of their largest contracts and very possibly cost him his job.

Early the next morning when he came into work, he was surprised to see other cars in the parking lot. When he got to his office, he found a few of the engineers already hard at work.

When he asked one of them what was going on, they told him, 'You know, it was the funniest thing. In all honesty I was kind of relieved when you told us we were giving up on this. I went home, saw my wife, had fun with my kids, and went to bed relaxed for the first time in a couple of months. Then I woke up around 3 a.m. with an idea completely different from what we've been exploring over the last six weeks. I thought I owed it to you to come in and run some numbers to test its viability, and to my surprise, a couple of the other engineers were already in here having had a similar "3 a.m." idea. I think this could actually work!'

Not only did it work, but the project came in on time and in budget. Don told me that he was proud of the team for pulling it off, but even prouder of the fact that they did it without the kind of 'hair on fire' stress that many companies used to try and boost productivity and results.

Years later, he went back to the company as a consultant and spoke with some of the engineers who had worked on that project. They said that 'giving up' had so become part of the company culture that whenever someone got really stuck, their colleagues would ask, 'Have you given up yet?'

Giving up always worked and they were always surprised when it did.

 Have you been overthinking some aspect of your impossible project? Try 'giving up' by taking the day off from thinking about it. Worst case, you'll get a break and some of your mental bandwidth back; best case, you'll be surprised and delighted when something new comes to mind!

How did you show up to your impossible project today?

What did you do? What did you notice? What happened?

DAY 60

How Much Time Do You Spend in the Unknown?

*'Most people are afraid of the unknown, so they
develop beliefs about things to make them feel safe.
I love the unknown, so I don't need beliefs.'*

MANDY EVANS

In the early part of the fifth century, a monk named Bodhidharma brought the teachings of Zen to China for the first time. He was invited to visit Emperor Wu of Liang, who was a great patron of Buddhism and had studied with his own teacher for many years.

The first question the emperor asked the monk was: 'What is the essence of your teaching?'

Bodhidharma's response was simply, 'Vast emptiness. Nothing holy.'

Now as the emperor was thought to be a god by his people, this was potentially very insulting, but he managed his anger and asked a second question: 'I have been a great patron of your religion and have built many monasteries – what merit has my generosity earned me?'

'No merit,' said Bodhidharma.

The now openly angry emperor spit out his third and final question: 'Who are you to say these things to me?'

'I don't know,' was Bodhidharma's honest reply.

One of the differences between Bodhidharma and the rest of us was that he was willing to admit he didn't know who he really was, while most of us fill our lives with activities and goals designed to 'prove' that we are who we say we are or aren't who we fear we are.

We don't like to admit that we don't know something. I once asked a client what she wanted to do about a particularly thorny situation in her business. Her response was, 'I can't answer that question — I don't know.' She had, of course, answered the question beautifully — it's just that 'I don't know' wasn't an acceptable answer for her.

It seems to me that the reason we struggle to find answers to the questions that matter most in our lives — questions like 'How do I handle this unexpected circumstance?' or 'What's the next step with my impossible project?' — is because we're not willing to stay in the unknown long enough to open up to the space inside — the space where we can access insights and revelations from our deeper wisdom.

This is true not just in our thinking, but also in our speaking. Each time we open our mouth to speak without already knowing what we're going to say, we open up to the possibility of saying something brilliant. Or of saying something 'stupid,' which is why so many of us run from the unknown with all the panic and grace of a character in a zombie movie.

Here's your question for today:

How much time do you spend hanging out in the unknown?

If you think you can't answer that question, consider the possibility that that answer is in and of itself the gateway to wisdom: 'I don't know.'

How did you show up to your impossible project today?

What did you do? What did you notice? What happened?

DAY 61

The Invisible Power of Insight

'A moment's insight is sometimes worth a life's experience.'
OLIVER WENDELL HOLMES

In their amazing book *Invisible Power*, consultants Ken Manning, Robin Charbit, and Sandra Krot share story after story of the impact a deeper understanding of the inside-out principles has on businesses. Here's one:

> We were asked to help a $5 billion-revenue biotech company address an earnings shortfall. Their plan for $600 million in EBIT [earnings before interest and tax] had been rejected; their holding company was requesting $700 million. They were a smart and resourceful organization that had achieved breakthrough results many times before, but this time they were stumped...

> As we started to share the inside-out nature of life and the participants' minds began to settle, we observed a wonderful phenomenon in the room. Although no one said it outright, there was a deep feeling of love and connection... The team ... quickly made the connection between their mutual openness and a reliable flow of new ideas. They instinctively saw that without mental constraints or fear, they could explore anything and be brilliant.

> Shortly after their realization, we moved into the problem-resolution phase of our program. Buoyed by their strong feeling of connection, the participants were able to listen to each other without the filters common in highly experienced people... Within a day and a half, they had collectively identified EBIT improvement ideas totaling over $400 million! This list was triaged into about $200 million of discrete projects that, when implemented, allowed the company to get very close to its earnings target that year.

The consultants go on to conclude:

Understanding how the mind works, and that it is only your thinking in the way of your creative capacity for out-of-the-box insight, enables teams to have synergy in the face of problems big and small. Every situation is an opportunity to engage with clarity and perspective and with the confidence that wise, productive thinking is always within reach.

Crises or seemingly impossible tasks may appear to be the catalyst to bring out the best in teams. But as we see it, when people understand their mental life and focus on what needs to be done, insights and new perspectives begin to flow.

Chances are the numbers you're dealing with in your impossible project are a little bit smaller than those in the case study I've just shared. But the principles shared in this book and their implications are not only life-changing on the outside, they can lead to an inner wealth that has value beyond measure.

How did you show up to your impossible project today?

What did you do? What did you notice? What happened?

DAY 62

Disempowering Yourself

'You have power over your mind – not outside events. Realize this, and you will find strength.'

MARCUS AURELIUS

I once did a coaching intensive with a self-described 'control freak' who was eager to master the inside-out understanding. She told me that she was willing to commit fully to the process and put every strategy I shared with her into immediate action. What I suggested instead was that she would benefit greatly from reading my new book, *Disempowering Yourself: A Guide to Letting Go*.

While I was joking, what I was trying to point out was that one of the main reasons people struggle to get insights into the nature of the human experience is that they think they have to struggle in order to get them. All breakthroughs come about via a shift in consciousness. And almost anything we do to try to make this kind of breakthrough happen actually gets in the way of it happening all by itself.

To better explain how these shifts in consciousness come about, I shared the metaphor of a hyperbaric chamber. While its efficacy as a healing modality is still a source of some debate, the idea of a hyperbaric chamber is simple. High volumes of oxygen are pumped into an air-tight chamber and any person within the chamber therefore absorbs more oxygen into their bloodstream. Proponents of this therapy claim that spending time in an oxygen-rich environment stimulates the body's natural healing capacity. Some athletes use hyperbaric chambers as a way of gaining greater strength, endurance, and clarity of mind. You don't need to actually do anything to get the benefits – just by hanging out in the chamber, your body naturally absorbs the oxygen.

It seems to me that creative breakthroughs work in much the same way, except the 'oxygen' in this case is the presence of the deeper energy and intelligence behind life – the invisible giant of the creative Mind.

When we tune into that presence within us, something inside us 'wakes up,' and we're able to take our enhanced clarity, heightened sense of wellbeing, and increased access to wisdom with us when we go back out into the 'real world.'

Today, why not disempower yourself? Most people initially balk at this idea, but I'm not suggesting that you abandon responsibility for your actions or go back to living life as a victim of your circumstances. It is simply that when you stop trying so hard to be the predominant creative force in your life, the natural creative force will begin to come through you more and more.

How did you show up to your impossible project today?

What did you do? What did you notice? What happened?

DAY 63

Rest, Review, Recharge, and Renew

'Each person holds so much power within themselves that needs to be let out. Sometimes they just need a little nudge, a little direction, a little support, a little coaching, and the greatest things can happen.'

PETE CARROLL

The Week in Review

- I put in the hours on my project:

  ☐   ☐

  Yes   No

- I let go:

  ☐   ☐   ☐   ☐

  Not at all   Rarely   Sometimes   Daily

What I did:

. . . .

. . . .

. . . .

What I noticed:

....

....

....

....

What happened:

....

....

....

....

BECOMING DISCOURAGEMENT-PROOF

'God, grant me the serenity to accept the things I cannot change, the courage to change the things I can, and the wisdom to know the difference.'

REINHOLD NIEBUHR

One of the great unsung truths of the human spirit is that it's always easier to 'get back up on the horse' than not to fall off in the first place. As we discussed in the first part of this book, the human spirit is made to bounce.

This week, we'll tap into our innate resilience and see how the only thing that can bring us down is the cumulative weight of our own discouraged thinking. Fortunately, we're never more than a thought away from being lifted up by hope, fresh thought, and infinite possibilities...

IMPOSSIBLE CHALLENGE NO.10: MADE TO BOUNCE

Pay particular attention to any feelings of discouragement or disappointment you experience this week. Mark down when you first notice the feelings, and again when you notice that your natural buoyancy and resilience have brought you back home to yourself.

DAY 64

The Hangover of Discouragement

'Fall down seven times; stand up eight.'
CHINESE PROVERB

I once had a client who spent the first two days of a three-day coaching intensive telling me why his life was awful and was sure to get even worse. Any alternative possibility I presented was quickly shot down by facts about the past or projections about the future.

By the end of the second day, somewhat exasperated, I said to him, 'I can tell you right now I see the possibility of a bright future for you, and I know for a fact you could be enjoying your life right now, today, this moment, regardless of what's going on. And you'd better hope that I'm right and you're wrong. Because if you're right, you're screwed; if I'm right, at least there's the possibility of better times ahead.'

Surprised and a bit taken aback by my outburst, he asked me what I thought he should do.

'You're going to have to find a way to shut the hell up in your mind,' I said, 'and listen for something new – something you don't already think and something you don't already "know." If you do, I promise you you'll hear something that'll change this for you.'

To his credit, he did, and he was a different person by the time he left at the end of the next day. His only complaint was that I hadn't told him to 'shut up' earlier.

If I had, we wouldn't have wasted so much airtime replaying the sound-bites and tape loops he'd been running in his head over the first two days. But that's just how the mind works – we live in the feeling of our 'right now' thinking, moment by moment by moment, and if it looks as though those feelings are coming from the outside world, we'll assume we'll be stuck with them.

One of my students shared the analogy of waking up with a terrible hangover. If she hadn't understood the nature of hangovers, she'd have genuinely thought she was dying. She might have taken the time to get her affairs in order, make peace with her unresolved conflicts and call an ambulance. But because she knew how hangovers worked, she took a couple of aspirin, promised herself that she'd never drink that much again (with her fingers crossed behind her back, obviously), and got on with her day, knowing that hangovers go away all by themselves as the amazing self-correcting mechanism of the body brings itself back to a healthy equilibrium.

Similarly, if we understand the nature of the mind, we know that when we feel miserable, bleak, and hopeless, it's because we're caught up in some miserable, bleak, and hopeless thinking. And we also know that the moment we put that thinking to one side, the amazing self-correcting mechanism of the mind will bring us some fresh new thinking and creative, hopeful possibilities as it restores itself once more to a healthy equilibrium.

In Alcoholics Anonymous, participants are encouraged to live in 'daytight compartments.' They don't need to give up their drug of choice or live positively forever — they need only do it 'just for today.'

What if, just for today, you let go of any discouragement you might be feeling about your impossible project and see what new thoughts, feelings, and possibilities come to mind?

How did you show up to your impossible project today?

What did you do? What did you notice? What happened?

DAY 65

No Pressure

'The really efficient laborer will be found not to crowd his day with work, but will saunter to his task surrounded by a wide halo of ease and leisure.'

HENRY DAVID THOREAU

During the 2016 Summer Olympics, I found myself unexpectedly caught up in the drama and artistry of the men's synchronized diving event. There was something about watching these athletes perform their carefully choreographed and endlessly practiced dives that captured my imagination.

While the Chinese men ultimately won the gold medal, it was the interviews with the American and British divers (silver and bronze medalists respectively) that really caught my attention. When asked about handling the pressure of performing very technical and physically demanding dives with millions of people watching, the American divers shared their coping strategies, while the British divers seemed a bit puzzled by the question.

'We've done these dives hundreds of times in our own pool,' one of them said. 'There's not really any extra pressure doing them in this pool.'

Another added words to the effect of 'Why would we feel pressure? We're just doing what we do every day.'

These statements staggered me, as they showed a level of insight into how the mind worked that I wasn't used to seeing out in the world. What these divers apparently realized was:

There is no pressure pre-existent in the world or inherently present in any given situation. The only pressure we can ever feel is 100 percent generated via Thought in our own mind.

Pressure is just a thought that comes and goes of its own accord. So why would we ever attempt to *increase* the amount of pressure that we feel? Why do we make our goals or deadlines more important than they are?

The reason, as best I can tell, is that we mistake the clarity, presence, and focused intention (i.e. 'flow') that often come while working towards a clear target or deadline with the pressure our thinking often generates as we do so.

Or to put it another way, we mistake correlation for causation. The fact that two things often occur in close proximity to each other doesn't mean that one causes the other. Firetrucks don't cause fires. Umbrellas don't cause rain. And pressure isn't an intrinsic or even essential element of high performance.

As you work on your impossible project this week, do it without intentionally putting any pressure on yourself to succeed, or even perform at your best. It's fine to want to do well, just not to threaten yourself with dire implications or feelings of regret and self-loathing if you don't.

If you do feel pressure, don't do anything to try to lessen it or talk yourself out of it. Just recognize that it's a feeling made out of the transient energy of Thought, and as such it will come and go of its own accord.

How did you show up to your impossible project today?

What did you do? What did you notice? What happened?

DAY 66

Where Confidence Comes From

'With realization of one's own potential and self-confidence in one's ability, one can build a better world.'

THE DALAI LAMA

When I started out teaching and speaking back in 1990, I knew I could 'manufacture' confidence by manipulating my physiology and programming my mind to imagine positive outcomes and experiences. In a way, I would pretend to be confident until I started to feel confident – the classic 'fake it 'til you make it' approach.

Later, as I mentioned earlier, I would plan and rehearse my talks meticulously until I felt confident in my material. I would even mentally rehearse dealing with all the things I could imagine coming up during the talk, from being asked a difficult question to being chased around the stage by a knife-wielding maniac. (I had quite the imagination...)

Then at some point, something dawned on me: I was only ever really nervous *before* I got in front of a group. Once I was engaged in what I was doing and connected to the people in the room, a sort of natural confidence and enjoyment came through me. This was true no matter how large the audience and even when I was asked questions that hadn't been part of my preparation. In fact, my favorite bits of the presentations were the demonstrations and Q&A, where I had no idea what would be coming at me or through me.

This realization was a game-changer. Instead of trying to make myself feel better when I got nervous, I allowed the nerves to come and go with my thinking, knowing that once my attention was off myself and back out into the world, my natural confidence would come through. And since I was at my best when I was fully engaged and present in the unknown, I stopped rehearsing and scenario planning.

At one recent multi-speaker event, I had to explain this to the event organizers, and the analogy that occurred to me was a sailboat. Understanding the physics of the world, we know that if we aim our boat in roughly the direction we want to go and unfurl our sails, the wind will arrive to take us there. There's not much value in paddling while we wait for the wind, and there's no value at all in trying to blow into the sails ourselves.

In the same way, all we ever need do in life is aim ourselves in a direction and 'unfurl our sails' by making ourselves as available as we can to the sometimes gentle and sometimes awesome force of our creative nature.

In this sense, confidence comes from understanding the physics of the mind — the 'wind' of fresh new thinking, the 'sails' of consciousness, and the buoyant 'ocean' of universal energy on which we sail.

What if you really could just show up and respond to what showed up, knowing that the invisible giant of the creative Mind would always show up with you?

How did you show up to your impossible project today?

What did you do? What did you notice? What happened?

DAY 67

Press On

*'Nothing in the world can take the place of persistence.
Talent will not; nothing is more common than unsuccessful
men with talent. Genius will not; unrewarded genius is
almost a proverb. Education will not; the world is full of
educated derelicts. Persistence and determination alone
are omnipotent. The slogan "press on" has solved and
always will solve the problems of the human race.'*

CALVIN COOLIDGE

I was speaking with a colleague recently who pointed out that persistence and resilience were the two most highly leveraged traits leading to success in the world.

Contrary to current business wisdom, these traits do not need to be acquired or practiced in order to be experienced. When we insightfully recognize the inside-out nature of experience, persistence and resilience emerge from underneath the 'noise' of our habitual inclination to hold ourselves back in order to avoid experiencing fear or discouragement.

Here's how I wrote about it in *The Inside-Out Revolution*:

We live in the feeling of our thinking, but because thought is largely invisible to us, we attribute those feelings to what we see around us.

Because we think that our fear is causally linked to certain specific life circumstances, we do everything we can to avoid and/or protect ourselves from those circumstances.

Because we think our happiness will come from getting what we want, we pursue success at all costs. If we don't get what we want, we feel discouraged and lose heart. But that feeling of discouragement has nothing to do with the results we are creating.

The moment we see the truth behind the thought/feeling system – that every feeling is just the shadow of a thought, and thoughts come and go when we let them – we stop being scared of our feelings and just feel them.

In short, when we come to see that fear and discouragement don't come from our *results* but from our *thinking*, we're less inclined to avoid challenges or the mistakes that make up our learning curve. We press on because we have no reason not to.

And when we don't stop ourselves, it's amazing what we can create along the way.

How did you show up to your impossible project today?

What did you do? What did you notice? What happened?

DAY 68

What to Do When
You Don't Know What to Do

*'If you just enjoy yourself, stop looking for any more,
you silence your mind to a state of no-thought. Then
divine thought comes in ... and you have the answer.'*

SYD BANKS

Were you ever told to 'count to 10' before speaking when you were angry or upset? Or to take a few deep breaths to gather yourself and regain your bearings before trying to solve a problem or resolve a conflict?

The reason these bits of advice are so common everywhere in the world is that they're rooted in a simple truth. It's the truth behind why we have our best ideas in the shower or while out for a walk, and why, no matter how smart we are at our best, we all behave like idiots from time to time.

Think of the mind as being like the ocean – continually changing on the surface, with hidden currents underneath, and absolute stillness underneath that. The wisdom that will guide us forward is already there underneath the waves of our personal thinking. The wisdom that will take us deeper is already there in the stillness and depths of our soul.

Which is why the most powerful way to use the mind is to listen.

Whenever we take the time to be quiet and just listen, it's amazing what comes through. We don't even need to ask a question – we can just let our thoughts settle and new ideas and insights bubble up into the space within.

This receptive capacity of the mind tends to be undervalued in our culture, but throughout history, the greatest thinkers and leaders have been the ones willing to do what researcher Cal Newport calls 'deep work' – escaping the constant noise of the world around them to reflect more deeply on the emergent wisdom within.

Today, may you rest in peace in the silence of your mind. May you enjoy yourself and stop looking for any more. And may the wisdom within you illuminate the world around you.

How did you show up to your impossible project today?

What did you do? What did you notice? What happened?

DAY 69

You Can Do Hard

'Life is not easy for any of us. But what of that? We must have perseverance and above all confidence in ourselves. We must believe that we are gifted for something, and that this thing, at whatever cost, must be attained.'

MARIE CURIE

I first heard the expression 'You can do hard' from one of my mentors, and I found it both self-evidently true and oddly comforting. While I'm a big fan of not turning difficulty into suffering, it's nice to know that when difficulty comes, the strength to handle it often comes too.

The poet Rudyard Kipling spoke to this dynamic in his poem *If*:

If you can keep your head when all about you
Are losing theirs and blaming it on you,
If you can trust yourself when all men doubt you,
But make allowance for their doubting too;
If you can wait and not be tired by waiting,
Or being lied about, don't deal in lies,
Or being hated, don't give way to hating,
And yet don't look too good, nor talk too wise:

If you can dream – and not make dreams your master;
If you can think – and not make thoughts your aim;
If you can meet with Triumph and Disaster

And treat those two impostors just the same;
If you can bear to hear the truth you've spoken
Twisted by knaves to make a trap for fools,
Or watch the things you gave your life to, broken,
And stoop and build 'em up with worn-out tools:

If you can make one heap of all your winnings
And risk it on one turn of pitch-and-toss,
And lose, and start again at your beginnings
And never breathe a word about your loss;
If you can force your heart and nerve and sinew
To serve your turn long after they are gone,
And so hold on when there is nothing in you
Except the Will which says to them: 'Hold on!'

If you can talk with crowds and keep your virtue,
Or walk with Kings – nor lose the common touch,
If neither foes nor loving friends can hurt you,
If all men count with you, but none too much;
If you can fill the unforgiving minute
With sixty seconds' worth of distance run,
Yours is the Earth and everything that's in it,
And – which is more – you'll be a Man, my son!

As you work on your impossible project, there'll be times where things don't go your way. You'll make mistakes, and sometimes be blamed for things that were nothing to do with you. None of that is indicative of your ability to succeed.

Regardless of gender, you have within you the will to hold on and the unfailing capacity to fill each minute with 'sixty seconds' worth of distance run.' It won't always be easy. You won't always win. You might even find it hard. But that's okay. You can do hard.

How did you show up to your impossible project today?

What did you do? What did you notice? What happened?

DAY 70

Rest, Review, Recharge, and Renew

'Let no feeling of discouragement prey upon you,
and in the end you are sure to succeed.'

ABRAHAM LINCOLN

The Week in Review

- I put in the hours on my project:

  ☐   ☐
  Yes   No

- I noted when I felt discouraged or disappointed and when I bounced back:

  ☐   ☐   ☐   ☐
  Not at all   Rarely   Sometimes   Daily

What I did:

....

....

....

....

What I noticed:

....

....

....

....

What happened:

....

....

....

....

THE HOME STRETCH

*'Whatever it takes to finish things, finish. You will
learn more from a glorious failure than you ever
will from something you never finished.'*
NEIL GAIMAN

You know how in a race with laps they ring the bell when it's the final lap? Well,
imagine me ringing the bell right now – ding, ding, ding, ding, ding!

If you're doing this 90-day program in real time, this week is the beginning of
the home stretch.

There are essentially three ways to finish out your 90 days:

1. Sprint to the finish.

2. Expand the game.

3. Ride the wave.

I'll take you through each of these three paths to success this week, along with a
couple of ideas you'll find helpful regardless of which path you choose to take...

IMPOSSIBLE CHALLENGE NO.11:
YOUR TURN:

Each day this week, give yourself a personal challenge. You can repeat something from elsewhere in the program or make up your own. The key is this:

- Choose something that you don't normally do but will genuinely benefit you if you do.

- Choose something that you'll actually do!

DAY 71

What Season Is It?

'Look to the seasons when choosing your cures.'
HIPPOCRATES

There is a rather poetic passage from the Bible that is perhaps better known as a lyric in a sixties rock song or from its somewhat tenuous appearance in both versions of the movie *Footloose*:

> *To everything, there is a season. And a time to every purpose under the heavens. A time to be born and a time to die. A time to plant and a time to pluck up that which is planted. A time to kill and a time to heal. A time to break down and a time to build up. A time to weep and a time to laugh. A time to mourn and a time to dance. [Hence its apparent relevance in* Footloose.*]*

> *A time to cast away stones and a time to gather stones together. A time to embrace and a time to refrain from embracing. A time to get and a time to lose. A time to keep and a time to cast away. A time to tear and a time to sew. A time to keep silence and a time to speak. A time to love and a time to hate. A time of war and a time of peace.*

How is this relevant to entering the home stretch of your impossible project?

We tend to think of flow in terms of continuous action. But another way of thinking about it is that it's simply doing the right thing at the right time. And in order to do that, we need to stay tuned into – and in tune with – the 'season' of our impossible project.

Does your impossible project need watering or does it need to be left alone? Does it need hard work and massive action or does it need more space and time to grow?

Do you need to stop talking about your impossible project for a while and let it take on its own life? Or do you need to start talking about it a lot more?

Your mission, should you choose to accept it, is simply to tune into your impossible project and get a sense of what it needs most right now. And then, of course, to give it what it needs.

How did you show up to your impossible project today?

What did you do? What did you notice? What happened?

DAY 72

Three Paths to Success

'Keep on going, and the chances are that you will stumble on something, perhaps when you are least expecting it. I never heard of anyone ever stumbling on something sitting down.'
CHARLES F. KETTERING

As I mentioned at the top of the week, there are basically three ways to finish out the program:

1. Sprint to the finish

In the early laps of a race, people are usually pacing themselves, but there comes a certain point where there's nothing left to save yourself for — you've just got to make your move and sprint to the finish.

If you choose to sprint to the finish with your project, your life/work balance may be a little bit out of whack over the next 20 days. The pace may not be sustainable over time. But that's okay. As the saying goes, 'You can rest when you're dead.' Or more realistically, in about three weeks' time.

(Having said that, tomorrow's lesson might be instructive as to how to take extra good care of yourself even as you're pushing yourself harder than ever before.)

2. Expand the game

Maybe even 20 consecutive days of sprinting isn't going to get your project done. But if you're still inspired (or more inspired than ever), you can 'expand the game' by either giving yourself more time (no, that's not cheating — we made up 90 days, remember?) or expanding the size and scope of your impossible dream.

If you choose to expand the game, Day 73 will offer you some useful tips and perspectives.

3. Ride the wave

Of course, you may decide to abandon all hope of reaching your goal and choose to ride the wave of energy that's come from throwing yourself into creating it. Even if all you've been doing is reading each day without doing any of the exercises, there'll be a certain amount of energy and momentum that's lifting you up like a wave.

If you choose to ride the wave, you're not going to drop out of the program, but you're going to let the creative intelligence and the energy of creation carry you forward and see where it takes you. (If you decide to ride the wave, you'll find Day 74 of particular interest.)

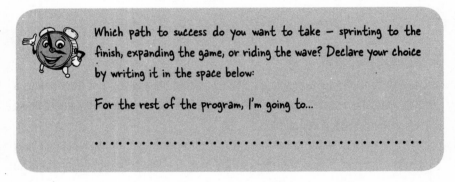

Which path to success do you want to take — sprinting to the finish, expanding the game, or riding the wave? Declare your choice by writing it in the space below:

For the rest of the program, I'm going to...

. . . .

How did you show up to your impossible project today?

What did you do? What did you notice? What happened?

DAY 73

The Art of Sprinting

*'If everything seems under control, you're
just not going fast enough.'*
MARIO ANDRETTI

People sometimes wonder how it is that some high achievers are able to get so much done and yet seem to take so much time off. What I've seen in the most balanced of the bunch is that they've learned 'the art of sprinting' – that is, how to give their all to a project and then rest, recover, relax and renew.

Here's a simple way of thinking about it:

Visualize a sprinter like Usain Bolt as he bursts across the finish line, chest held high and looking as if he could do it all over again with a minute or two of rest. Then, by way of contrast, bring to mind images of marathon runners collapsing the moment they cross the finish line, needing to be wrapped in foil blankets to prevent them going into hypothermic shock.

One reason for the difference is to do with the sheer level of physical exertion, but sports psychologist James Loehr suggests another reason is that while a marathoner can't see 26 miles into the future, a sprinter can always see the finish line just in front of them.

We can all give 100 percent of our focus and energy to something for a limited period of time, and we all struggle to produce that level of engagement and intensity when we don't know if we're going to need to sustain it for five minutes, five days, or five years.

When you see your project (or work or marriage or pretty much anything) as a marathon, you tend to conserve your energy. You always want to make sure you've got something in the tank for later. One milestone begins to blend into the next, and while you might find yourself in 'the zone' from time to time, you're more likely to find yourself zoned out and daydreaming about getting out of 'the rat race' and spending your days pretty much anywhere else than wherever it is you happen to be.

When you see your project as a series of sprints, you are able to give your all for short bursts. You train, focus, and then when you're done, you're done. The key to your success is building plenty of 'quality recovery time' into your schedule.

The point is this: you can do a lot more than you think you can in a much shorter period of time if you're willing to build a routine designed around periods of intense activity followed by periods of quality recovery time.

So, today:

- Choose an aspect of your impossible project that you would like to be able to give your all to, even though you are concerned about the toll it might take on your health, relationships or life.

- Now, design a 'sprinting' routine that will be sustainable for the rest of the program. Your impossible project already has a finish line, so simply make sure that each unit of activity is balanced out by an equal and opposite period of rest and recovery.

- Go for it! Know that you will probably have to adjust your routine as you go, but never increase the intensity or duration of your activity without also increasing the quality and duration of your recovery time.

How did you show up to your impossible project today?

What did you do? What did you notice? What happened?

DAY 74

Expanding the Game

'You will either step forward into growth
or you will step back into safety.'
ABRAHAM MASLOW

Here's a drawing I was first shown by a management consultant almost two decades ago:

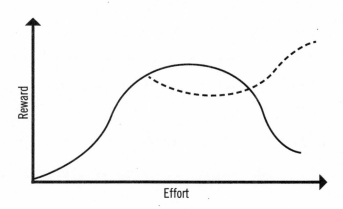

The basic bell-shaped curve is probably one you're already familiar with. It's sometimes called a Bandura curve, and it's often used to illustrate the relationship between effort and reward.

When you first begin a project, your efforts don't bring about much reward. Then, as you carry on up the curve, they start bringing more and more reward, and that goes up and up and up, and then you get to a point at which you have got the maximum reward for the effort. Then the law of diminishing returns kicks in and it's all downhill from there.

But if you expand the game and launch the next part of your project before you've 'peaked,' a new curve forms. By 'jumping' before you reach the point of maximum reward, you carry the momentum of what you've done so far with you into the next adventure (or next phase of the same adventure).

This is different from being 'flighty' or 'never seeing anything through.' It's neither an arbitrary change in direction nor an 'avoidance of success.' It's just a way of taking advantage of what you've done so far to help propel you to the next level.

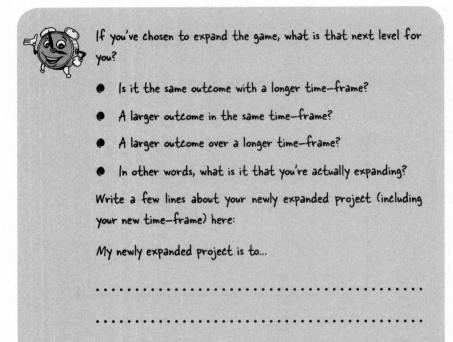

If you've chosen to expand the game, what is that next level for you?

● Is it the same outcome with a longer time-frame?

● A larger outcome in the same time-frame?

● A larger outcome over a longer time-frame?

● In other words, what is it that you're actually expanding?

Write a few lines about your newly expanded project (including your new time-frame) here:

My newly expanded project is to...

. . . .

. . . .

. . . .

How did you show up to your impossible project today?

What did you do? What did you notice? What happened?

DAY 75

Riding the Wave

*'No matter how hard a surfer works, the ocean
is doing most of the heavy lifting.'*
CLARENCE THOMPSON

When you started out, your impossible project was designed around creating a particular result in the world. But by this point in the game, you may have realized that you don't particularly care about that result. You flirted with it, you went on a few dates, you may even have gotten engaged, but marriage just isn't on the cards with this particular project. So instead of sprinting to the finish or expanding the game, a more appropriate way forward may be to 'ride the wave.'

Now in the spirit of full disclosure, I have tried to surf exactly twice in my life. The first time, when I was a kid, I was able to stand up briefly before falling down and being threatened by a bunch of bigger kids because I was apparently on their ocean. The second time, I didn't even stand up.

What I've learned from the actual surfers in my life is that riding the wave is an extremely engaged process. You're not passively allowing the wave to take you, you're actively engaging with your environment at all times in order to stay balanced as you ride. And the best surfers have a sixth sense about which waves are worth riding and which are worth letting go past. As each wave gets closer, they make the call whether to let it lift them up and drop them back down or to stand up and engage with it. They're not trying to control what comes – they're taking what the ocean gives them and seeing where it takes them.

In the same way, choosing to ride the wave down the home stretch of your impossible project means staying tuned in, present to the daily sessions, present to life, and present to the movement of the creative intelligence inside you, so you start to develop a sixth sense about which waves of thought you're going to let flow past and which waves of opportunity you're going to stand up and ride. And then you're going to see where they take you.

 Choose your own metaphor for 'riding the wave.' Do you have an example from your own life of engaging fully with what's happening without having a particular destination in mind?

How did you show up to your impossible project today?

What did you do? What did you notice? What happened?

DAY 76

The Goldilocks Principle

'Psychology is action, not thinking about oneself.'
ALBERT CAMUS

A client complained to me recently that he needed to become more disciplined, as he was failing to hit his targets in several key areas of his business. Earlier in my career I might have taken his complaint seriously and worked with him on becoming 'a more disciplined person,' even taking the time to explore his patterns of self-sabotage and encouraging him to 'just try harder' and 'focus more' on what he really wanted. But it's become clearer and clearer to me over the years that success is less a matter of becoming a different kind of person than of finding what already works well for us and doing more of it. I call this 'the Goldilocks principle.'

There's always a way of doing things that fits just right for you. Do you think you're too lazy to succeed? Consider Marc Allen, the millionaire publisher behind such personal development classics as *Creative Visualization* and *The Power of Now*. I had to get special permission to interview him for my radio show at 11 a.m. one week, as he normally won't do anything remotely business related until after lunch, a habit he developed long before he achieved his financial success.

Assume you're not tough enough to make it in the dog-eat-dog world of business? Self-proclaimed 'hippie ice-cream entrepreneurs' Ben Cohen and Jerry Greenfield get round this by getting an imaginary entity they call 'the monster' to make their difficult business decisions for them. As Ben reputedly told Jerry when economic realities made it necessary for them to let employees go, 'The monster is hungry – the monster must eat!'

The point is, you can either try to adapt yourself to fit in to what you think of as the 'right way' to do something or you can employ the Goldilocks principle and find a way to do it that is 'just right' for you.

How could you apply the 'Goldilocks principle' to the final stages of your impossible project? What approach would work beautifully for you, even if no one else would ever think to (or want to) do it that way?

How did you show up to your impossible project today?

What did you do? What did you notice? What happened?

DAY 77

Rest, Review, Recharge, and Renew

'When I am finishing a picture, I hold some God-made object up to it – rock, a flower, the branch of a tree or my hand – as a final test. If the painting stands up beside a thing man cannot make, the painting is authentic.'

MARC CHAGALL

The Week in Review

• I put in the hours on my project:

☐   ☐

Yes   No

• I set myself a personal challenge:

☐   ☐   ☐   ☐

Not at all   Rarely   Sometimes   Daily

What I did:

. . . .

. . . .

. . . .

What I noticed:

....

....

....

....

What happened:

....

....

....

....

THE ELEVENTH HOUR

'There is an immeasurable distance
between "late" and "too late."'

OG MANDINO

The expression 'the eleventh hour' dates all the way back to Shakespeare. It's almost the end, but not quite. There's still time to change the game. If you've decided to 'sprint to the finish' (and even if you haven't), our daily sessions this week are designed as potential game-changers – things that could catapult your project forward and/or turbo-boost it across the finish line.

That doesn't mean this needs to be a high-adrenaline week. After all, when the odds are really stacked against you, there's nothing to lose, so it's easier than ever to play to win...

IMPOSSIBLE CHALLENGE NO.12:
THE BIG ASK, REVISITED

Make the biggest ask of the entire program this week. Make an action request that would totally change the course of your project (and maybe even your life). You can re-read Day 33 for a reminder of what turns a 'big ask' into a simple request!

DAY 78

The Finish-Line Phenomenon

*'Depend on it sir, when a man knows he is to be hanged
in a fortnight, it concentrates his mind wonderfully.'*

SAMUEL JOHNSON

When I worked in the theater, I was always fascinated by what happened between the final dress rehearsal and opening night. With less than 24 hours to go, sets would be rebuilt, lighting cues changed, and new lines written and learned. It's the same everywhere. Marathon runners go into another gear as the finish line approaches; American football players find an extra burst of speed as they approach the end zone. And if you've ever had to pull an all-nighter to meet a study or work deadline, you'll know that we all find 'something extra' when we need it most. But where does this come from?

In his research into the psychology of happiness and success, positive psychologist Shawn Achor identified the point at which the brain releases higher than normal amounts of endorphins, dopamine, and other chemicals as 'the X-spot.' This internally generated chemical boost is what provides the extra energy needed for a sprint to the finish.

Even though as creators, our 'finish line' isn't always clearly defined, we can still benefit from finding the X-spot by realizing that what actually triggers that burst of chemicals isn't the finish line itself, but the hopeful thinking that finish line engenders.

The other thing that helps us out as we approach the finish line of our projects is an inevitable simplification of priorities.

In the 2015 movie *The Revenant*, Leonardo DiCaprio plays a man with only one thing on his mind — to get revenge on the man who killed his son. While we can debate the worthiness of the intention, the simplicity of focus carries him and his half-dead body over miles of treacherous terrain and past hundreds of pretty treacherous people.

More positively, great creators use single-minded focus to great effect when they lose themselves in the process of creation as they approach the finish line of their next project.

How do we incorporate the 'finish-line phenomenon' into our own creative process? By allowing ourselves to drop everything but the task at hand from our mental to-do list each time we enter into the studio, office, or arena.

 What actions would you take today if you could actually see the finish line of your impossible project approaching? What would you focus on and what would you feel free to ignore, at least for the next week or two?

How did you show up to your impossible project today?

What did you do? What did you notice? What happened?

DAY 79

Against All Odds

*'We are here to laugh at the odds and live our lives
so well that Death will tremble to take us.'*
CHARLES BUKOWSKI

Here's a story from David Key, a participant in one of our online 'Creating the Impossible' programs, who expanded and completed his project 'against all odds':

> When I first began the program, I recognized that ... you had to choose something with at least an 80 percent likelihood of failure... I didn't see myself as especially creative, so thought this would be a breeze. (How hard can it be to fail, after all?) As it turned out, the first thing I learned was that dreaming up the impossible was not as easy as I'd imagined. Then, at the eleventh hour, the idea came to me...

> Sitting with the family around the dinner table one Sunday, I bemoaned the fact that old-fashioned gravy boats were too wide. The gravy sits there on the dining table and by the time you've got the meat carved, it has cooled down from exposure to the air. Looking on the Internet, I discovered that many people had tried to tackle this problem over the years, but nobody really seemed to have cracked it. What was needed, I thought, was something with a lid, like a teapot, but for gravy. My wife, Anna, piped up, 'A g-pot!'

> I had my impossible goal. I would create a new kind of gravy boat, and see it on the shelves in a top department store, all in 90 days!

> Do you believe in blind coincidence? Within the first six weeks, I met a series of people who helped me to realize my dream, from a designer to a patent attorney to a buyer from John Lewis department store, all of whom loved the

idea and helped me to turn it into a reality. Throughout the process, the right people seemed to pop up at the right time, as if by magic. (Well, it does look like a magic lamp!)

My 80 percent odds of 'failure' seemed to be going into freefall. While the process took closer to six months than 90 days, the Gpot® became a reality.

What did I learn? That our thinking about a goal or project can actually be the one thing that gets in the way of our achieving it.

(You can get your very own Gpot® at www.gpot.co.uk)

How did you show up to your impossible project today?

What did you do? What did you notice? What happened?

DAY 80

A Formula for Miracles

'All miracles involve a shift in perception.'
A COURSE IN MIRACLES

In his book *The Enlightened Gardener Revisited*, Syd Banks shared his formula for how our personal reality is created:

Mind + Consciousness + Thought = Reality

As we explored in Chapter 1, *Mind* was Syd's word to describe the innate intelligence inside us – what I have been describing as 'the invisible giant.' *Consciousness*, in this context, is the space within which our experience unfolds. And *Thought* is the creative force – the creator of the content of what we think and feel.

In *The Inside-Out Revolution*, I extrapolated Syd's formula to take into account how miraculous new realities are created:

Mind + Consciousness + New Thought = New Reality

We now have a 'formula for miracles.' As I've said elsewhere in this book, it's 100 percent reliable. It's just that it's 98 percent unpredictable exactly what form that new thought and concurrent new reality will take.

How does that play out in terms of experiencing miracles in the creation of our impossible project, even at the eleventh hour? What can we do to help the process along?

- *Step One:* Start moving in the direction of what we want.

- *Step Two:* Notice what new possibilities show up in our mind and what new opportunities show up in our world.

- *Step Three:* Move forward with the stuff we're inclined to move forward with and leave the rest behind.

In a way, this formula takes us to a fork in the road between the path of linear cause and effect and the path of miracles. The path of linear productivity is the path of simple cause and effect, where we think that *If I do these things I will get this result.* While this can work out in the realm of the possible, when it comes to creating the impossible, it's not going to cut it.

But if we take the road less travelled, the path of effortless productivity, we sacrifice the predictability of linear cause and effect for the possibility of miracles. We don't know what twists and turns the path might take and we can't predict what's coming. But we do know it will take us to places we could never get to in any other way.

 If a miracle happened tonight and the successful completion of your impossible project was in reach, what's the very first thing you would notice when you woke up tomorrow morning? How would things be different?

How did you show up to your impossible project today?

What did you do? What did you notice? What happened?

DAY 81

Who Cares What You're Afraid Of?

*'That voice inside your head is not the voice of
God – it just sounds like it thinks it is.'*

CHERI HUBER

For many years, I made my living by helping people manage fear by confronting it, conquering it, lessening it, and eliminating it through a variety of tools and techniques. In all that time, the most consistently effective 'tool' I stumbled across was a simple question that I asked myself and my clients *ad nauseum*: 'What would you do if you weren't afraid?'

In other words, the most effective technique I had for dealing with fear involved ignoring it completely and carrying on as if it wasn't there. I can now see that the reason this worked so well was that unless there is a clear and present danger, the feeling of fear isn't telling us anything we particularly need to know.

When you're thinking scary thoughts about the future, you'll feel scared; when you're not thinking scary thoughts about the future, you won't. To the extent that you can see you're living in the feeling of the energy of Thought in the moment, neither one of those scenarios is remotely problematic.

What would you do today to create your impossible project if fear was telling you about your thinking, not your chances of success?

What would you do to create your impossible project if you weren't afraid?

How did you show up to your impossible project today?

What did you do? What did you notice? What happened?

DAY 82

The Results Accelerator

*'Only those who will risk going too far can
possibly find out how far it is possible to go.'*

T.S. ELIOT

Years ago I had the good fortune to help Paul McKenna research and edit his book on wealth creation, the aptly named *I Can Make You Rich*. Of all the millionaires and billionaires we interviewed in the process of putting the book together, the one who probably made the biggest impression on me was Sir Philip Green.

While in recent times Sir Philip has been the subject of much controversy, at the time of our interview with him he had just purchased over 100 shops in the Canary Islands. When he mentioned in passing that he hadn't actually been out there to look at them, Paul said, 'Isn't that risky?'

Sir Philip immediately replied, 'It's a *calculated* risk, but it's not risky.'

He went on to explain that he knew that the land that the shops were on was worth nearly as much as he'd paid for them. Even if the shops themselves didn't prove to be financially viable, he was actually only risking a small amount of money despite the large purchase price. The potential upside far outweighed the potential downside; consequently, it made sense to give it a go.

In a sense, taking a calculated risk is a results accelerator, opening up the possibility of reaching the desired end goal of our impossible project much more quickly and easily than we otherwise would. The question of course, is how you calculate the risk. Here's how:

- Take away all the imaginary risk about how bad you'll feel if your project fails, or how embarrassed you'll be if people judge you or laugh at you. (And point. It's always worse in my head when they laugh and point.) Because you know those feelings are made of thought and will come and go with your thinking, they don't have to be part of your calculation.

- Look at what is actually at stake as opposed to what's at stake in your nightmare scenario.

  Paul and I thought Sir Philip Green was risking tens of millions, when he knew his actual risk was well within his means. If you were to take a risk to make your impossible dream come true, what would be the actual amount at stake in terms of time, money, or any other commodity you would be putting into play?

- What can you do to limit or offset the risk?

  I've never really been much of a stock trader, but in my brief flirtation with the markets I discovered a wonderful thing called a 'stop loss,' which means you can actually pre-set the maximum amount of money you're willing to lose.

  While there may not be an actual 'stop loss' available with your impossible project, ways to limit the risk will come to mind when you put your creative intelligence to work on the question.

While I'm not going to pretend that this is an exhaustive study of risk analysis (and am certainly not recommending gambling or even investing in the stock market), I do want to point to the possibility that if you were willing to take a calculated risk, there might be things you could do that would dramatically increase the odds of achieving your project in the final week and/or the speed at which you could achieve your expanded project.

- What three things (at least) could you do today that would dramatically increase the speed at which you could create your impossible project?
- What would actually be at risk if you did them?
- Would it be worth it?

How did you show up to your impossible project today?

What did you do? What did you notice? What happened?

DAY 83

Going All In

'What is the point of being alive if you don't at least try to do something remarkable?'

JOHN GREEN

Metaphysical self-empowerment is based on the idea that 'If it's to be, it's up to me.' For years, I found this a comforting idea, because it made me feel less at the mercy of a seemingly fickle and at times almost random universe. But it also led to an incredible amount of pressure, stress, and self-doubt, as the fate of the world was a heavy load to carry on my relatively modest shoulders.

Over time, I noticed something interesting – each time life didn't deliver what I demanded of it, I relaxed a little bit more on the inside. My feelings of failure would quickly turn to a sense of ease and presence, and I would temporarily drop out of my role as emperor of the universe and go back to being an ordinary guy doing his best to make his way in the world.

This unempowered non-victim approach to life has served me well over the years. Each time I'm reminded that I don't control the universe, I remember that I don't need to. I can let all that thinking about how things are going to turn out drop away and simply do my best. It's a kind of 'positive fatalism' – a recognition that while the results I want may or may not be on the cards, throwing myself into creating them is the best and most enjoyable game in town.

What allows me to 'go all in' even when the odds seem stacked against me is my faith in the incredible creative potential of the deeper Mind. I rely on that creative force when I do live radio, when I show up to the blank page and write, and when I coach and teach. Each time it brings what's wanted and needed to the surface. In fact, every time I get myself out of the way, my deeper Self comes through. And each time I rely on the responsive intelligence of the deeper Mind to see me through, the more reliable it proves itself to be.

As our penultimate week comes to a close, take some time to reflect on these questions:

- What would you attempt if you knew you didn't have to be unhappy about failing?

- What would 'going all in' look like in the final week of your impossible project?

- What would it look like today?

- Are you all in?

How did you show up to your impossible project today?

What did you do? What did you notice? What happened?

DAY 84

Rest, Review, Recharge, and Renew

'Failures are finger posts on the road to achievement.'

C.S. LEWIS

The Week in Review

- I put in the hours on my project:

☐   ☐

Yes   No

- I made the biggest ask I could — one that could totally change the course of my project:

☐   ☐

Yes   No

What I did:

. . . .

. . . .

. . . .

. . . .

What I noticed:

....

....

....

....

What happened:

....

....

....

....

WEEK 13

YOUR LIFE AS A CREATOR

*'What you spend years building may be
destroyed overnight. Build anyway.'*

KENT M. KEITH

Creating isn't necessarily something we do 'because of' — it's something we can do 'in spite of.' We can create in spite of how we're feeling, in spite of everything else that's going on, in spite of what other people think about what we do and what we think about what other people think about what we do.

And that's the freedom of it. We're not dependent on being in a particular state of mind, we're not dependent on the world making space for us, and we're not dependent on circumstances aligning so that things work perfectly.

As we begin our final week together in this program, it's a great time to reflect on what you've learned even as you put the finishing touches on what you are creating...

IMPOSSIBLE CHALLENGE NO.13:
CREATING FROM NOTHING

For our final impossible challenge, we're going to go back to the very first exercise I shared with you in this book. Each day this week, create something from nothing. You can share your creations on social media with the hashtag # DailyCreation.

DAY 85

Falling in Love with Nothing

'In creating, the only hard thing is to begin.'
JAMES RUSSEL LOWELL

The basic premise of this book is that everything comes from nothing. And what we've been doing throughout this program is getting better at bringing things from the formless world into the world of form — creating 'some thing' from 'no thing.' We've been playing with the very essence of creation.

But one of the problems with beginning to create more consciously and consistently is that we get used to starting from something as often as from nothing. We have the idea for a book and then we develop the theme of that book. We have the kernel of a painting and then we develop that painting. We have the beginnings of a project and then we develop that project. And so we get used to showing up and having our next steps pre-scripted and pre-scribed. It can feel almost as though we've been given our marching orders before the day even begins and we just have to follow them.

While that can be a wonderful part of the creative process, if we get too comfortable in that stage, we can begin to lose our comfort with the unknown. And if we're not as in love with nothing as we are with something, we're going to struggle. The next time we think about creating something from scratch, we're going to put it off. Until eventually we never get around to creating anything.

What's the solution?

 Go out of your way to start from scratch this week. Begin again. Go back to the drawing board. Start from nothing. Find a blank page and begin to create. Show up and see what happens!

How did you show up to your impossible project today?
What did you do? What did you notice? What happened?

DAY 86

Enjoying Pretty Much Anything

'Learning is pleasurable, but doing is the height of enjoyment.'
NOVALIS

Many years ago I was co-leading a group of people with my friend and mentor Bill Cumming in a weekend workshop we called 'The Big Chat.' We set it up as a place to explore the big questions in life and create big games to play and impossible goals to reach.

During the exploration, several people in the group stumbled across a fearful thought that was limiting their vision of what was possible and driving a lot of their behavior around their work. While each one worded it slightly differently, it went something like this: 'If I don't achieve my impossible goal, I'll have to spend the rest of my life stuck in a horrible job doing stuff I really don't want to do.'

While we could have disputed the thought, changed it into its positive opposite, or simply let it go and waited for something better to come along, Bill took things in a different direction.

'What if,' he suggested, 'there's no such thing as a horrible job? Imagine that you went to work behind the counter of a fast-food restaurant. If you turned up each day having chosen to greet each customer and each task with energy, enthusiasm, and as if you had the most important job in the world, couldn't you turn even that job into a delight?'

When we tried that thought experiment, we soon saw that our enjoyment of any given job was far more a function of whether or not we threw ourselves into it with unreasonable enthusiasm than of the nature of the job itself.

That's not to say that you need to stay in a situation just because theoretically you could find a way to enjoy it. But it's probably worth acknowledging that if people like Viktor Frankl could find meaning and even moments of peace and beauty in a concentration camp, chances are you and I could find a way to enjoy working in a fast-food restaurant. And if we throw ourselves into any situation with wild abandon (or at least without a pile of miserable expectations), we'll find ourselves enjoying it whether we mean to or not.

Today, instead of cranking through your 'to do' list for your impossible project, just show up and do what's next as if it were the only thing you had to do today and the most important job in the world.

When and if you complete it, you can move on to the next thing on your list. Enjoy!

How did you show up to your impossible project today?

What did you do? What did you notice? What happened?

DAY 87

My Favorite Day

'Time you enjoy wasting is not wasted time.'
MARTHE TROLY-CURTIN

No lesson today, just a simple assignment:

 Go back through the first 12 weeks of this program and pick out your favorite day – the day that, for whatever reason, inspired you, moved you, got you off your butt, got you back onto your butt, or just did something for you that you want to take forward.

Re-read the day, redo the homework if there was any, and of course, don't forget to bring at least one thing into the world that didn't exist at the beginning of the day!

How did you show up to your impossible project today?

What did you do? What did you notice? What happened?

DAY 88

Living from the Inside Out

*'We can make our minds so like still water that beings
gather about us that they may see, it may be, their
own images, and so live for a moment with a clearer,
perhaps even with a fiercer life because of our quiet.'*

W.B. YEATS

I once sat down with a potential client who had read *The Inside-Out Revolution* and thought I'd be the perfect coach to help her make a difficult career transition. But at one point she got so frustrated with my unwillingness to provide her with a clear step-by-step action plan that she yelled, 'Just tell me what to *@#ing do and I'll do it!'

This also sometimes happens when I do introductory talks or interviews about the principles behind the inside-out understanding. People ask, 'What would the inside-out approach to weight loss/happiness/relationships/business building/or indeed any other potential aim or category of life experience be?'

The reason my answers are rarely initially satisfying is simple:

**The inside-out understanding is not an approach to life; it's an
understanding of what life is and how it works.**

By way of illustration, three commonly known forces at play in the physical world are electricity, magnetism, and gravity. Knowing these forces exist in nature does not imply any particular morality or course of action — it just makes it easier for us to navigate the physical world.

Similarly, knowing that there is a pre-existing intelligence (Mind), a built-in capacity for awareness and understanding (Consciousness), and an infinite creative potential continually creating our experience of reality (Thought) doesn't tell us what brand of beer to drink or how best to go about creating things in the world. It simply makes it easier for us to understand where our experience of life is coming from and who and what we really are.

'But if I want to get stuff done in the world,' you might say, 'what's the value of this understanding?'

You might also ask, 'Why is it that pretty much anyone who stays in the inside-out conversation long enough begins to find themselves happier, more successful, and in better relationships with the people around them?'

The answer to both is that the more accurately you see reality, the easier it is to navigate that reality.

Often our dreams and visions for a positive future come to us at seemingly low points in our lives. We've been almost forced to go inside and take stock – to find out what we know to be true beneath the constant noise of our habitual thinking. This deeper knowing never comes with feelings of anger or fear. It carries with it a feeling of resolve, and of hope, and of love, and of peace. We may not know how things are going to change, but we know we will be an agent of that change.

We don't need to be angry to make a difference – in fact, it's one of the least efficient ways of doing so. Anger may get people to gather in the street, but it's inspiration that gets them to march forward instead of mobbing up and destroying whatever they see around them.

And, we don't have to inspire ourselves either. We just have to be available for inspiration when it comes.

In a way, that's what this whole program has been about – learning, in the words of St. François de Sales, 'not to hinder the course of inspiration, not refusing consent when God's grace swells the sails of our soul, but receiving the gale, consenting to its motion and letting our ship sail under it, not hindering it by our resistance.'

How did you show up to your impossible project today?

What did you do? What did you notice? What happened?

DAY 89

Four Questions

*'I think I mainly climb mountains because I get a great deal
of enjoyment out of it. I never attempt to analyze these
things too thoroughly, but I think that all mountaineers
do get a great deal of satisfaction out of overcoming
some challenge which they think is very difficult for
them, or which perhaps may be a little dangerous.'*

Sir Edmund Hillary

As our program comes to an end, I'd like to encourage you to use today to look back over the last 90 days by answering the questions listed below and reflecting on your answers.

● What have you done?

What have you actually done over the last 90 days? What are the most significant actions you've taken, requests you've made, and relationships you've forged in the creation of your impossible project? How has what you've seen influenced what you've done?

● What was created?

What has come from those actions? What exists in the world now that didn't exist 90 days ago, apart from as a thought in your head?

- What was your role in its creation?

  How much of what happened seems as though it came about as a direct result of the actions you took? How much of what happened seems like luck? How much of what happened seems to have come from the invisible giant of the creative mind? How much seems like the result of 'Providence moving too'?

- What have you noticed?

  What have you come to see over the course of this program about yourself? What have you noticed about the process of creation? What has surprised you? What do you make of that?

Take some time over this, because once you've begun, more and more things will occur to you throughout the day...

How did you show up to your impossible project today?

What did you do? What did you notice? What happened?

DAY 90

Commencement

'On certain mornings, as we turn a corner,
an exquisite dew falls on our heart
and then vanishes.
But the freshness lingers, and this, always,
is what the heart needs.
The earth must have risen in just such a light
the morning the world was born.'

ALBERT CAMUS

The author Elizabeth Stone once wrote, 'Making the decision to have a child – it is momentous. It is to decide forever to have your heart go walking around outside your body.'

I feel the same way about everything I create. While many projects never come to fruition, the ones that do are eternally precious to me, regardless of whether or not they ever 'make it' in the world. They are like snapshots in time, reminding me of a particular dance with the creative potential.

But as I've begun to live my life from the creative intelligence within me more and more, I've become far less interested in what I create and far more interested in *creating*. Each time we create, we begin with a sense of infinite possibility. Specific results inevitably emerge along the way, but our experience of being both source and resource, mother and father, midwife and wet nurse to our creations is ours to keep.

So, as we bring our time together to a close, I want to congratulate you on coming this far and remind you that you've only just begun.

Here's the best news of all:

As we wake up to our deeper nature and true creative potential, our real life turns out to be even better than the life of our dreams.

How did you show up to your impossible project today?

What did you do? What did you notice? What happened?

Epilogue
Some Final Thoughts

'May you live in interesting times.'

CHINESE PROVERB

The week I began working on this book, I read a distressing (to me) article about how Mahatma Gandhi was estranged from his eldest son, Harilal, throughout his adult life. I immediately called my own first born, Oliver, and shared with him how much I loved him and that if it ever came down to it, I would choose my relationship with him over 'establishing a free and united India.'

Oliver went quiet for a few moments and then responded, 'Dad, we're fine. Go save India.'

We live in a world that is as socially and politically divided as at any point in my lifetime. Diseases like cancer and AIDS have claimed more lives in the past 50 years than the 'black death' of the bubonic plague killed in the 14th century.

Will we ever find a way to make sure every man, woman, and child goes to bed with food in their stomach? A cure for disease? A world where feelings of stress, pressure, and exhaustion seem more like minor mental illnesses than the inevitable side-effects of a life well-lived?

How can we improve the health of our loved ones and the health of the planet, physically, socially, and economically?

Is there any point in even trying?

It seems far from coincidental to me that in the past few days, as I've been reflecting on how to bring this book to a close, three separate people asked me what the core message of the book is – the one thing they need to know if they want to create the impossible in their own life and work.

One was a college student; one a budding rapper; one an already-successful musician.

The student wanted to know how she could bring about an end to racism; the budding rapper to understand how to overcome his reluctance to commit to moving forward with his career; the musician how to sell over a million records in a world where all the traditional distribution routes have disappeared or changed beyond recognition.

Fortunately, the answer for each of them was the same: *When it comes to any impossible project, the 'how' is almost always revealed to us along the way, and almost never visible when we begin.*

The reason something looks impossible is precisely because we can't see any way for it to come about. So to keep trying to figure out how something will happen before diving in and creating it is like continually looking for the Eiffel Tower when you're nowhere near Paris. What you can't see is far more a function of where you're standing than how hard you're looking.

So if you're wondering how to bring about social justice, your answer will be found in the process of working towards social justice. If you want to know how to advance your career, the answer(s) will arise as you engage more fully in the very next step that occurs to you to take. And whether you want to sell a million records, find a cure for cancer, win an Oscar, launch a new business, bring about an end to social inequality, feed the planet, or 'save India,' the 'how' will become apparent only when you step into the arena and begin.

As former US president Theodore Roosevelt famously said:

> *'It is not the critic who counts; not the man who points out how the strong man stumbles, or where the doer of deeds could have done them better. The credit belongs to the man who is actually in the arena, whose face is marred by dust and sweat and blood; who strives valiantly; who errs, who comes short again and again, because there is no effort without error and shortcoming;*

but who does actually strive to do the deeds; who knows great
enthusiasms, the great devotions; who spends himself in a
worthy cause; who at the best knows in the end the triumph of
high achievement, and who at the worst, if he fails, at least fails
while daring greatly, so that his place shall never be with those
cold and timid souls who neither know victory nor defeat.'

Or in the words of Marianne Williamson:

'God heard us. He sent help. He sent you.'

With all my love,

Michael

Appendix

The 'Creating the Impossible'
Seven-Day Online Jumpstart

I've created a set of seven videos to help you create momentum on your impossible project right out of the gate. You can do them in conjunction with the first seven days of the 90-day program, or use them to jumpstart your own self-created project plan.

To access the videos, go to:

http://www.michaelneill.org/cti/jumpstart

You'll be asked to register your name, email address, and the book's ISBN number (located on the back cover) for easy access!

Acknowledgments

'I love deadlines. I love that whooshing
sound they make as they go by.'
Douglas Adams

In the 25 years or so between my first writing job and this book, I have written and edited over a dozen full-length manuscripts and over 1,000 articles and blog posts without ever once missing a deadline. Perhaps in some harebrained attempt to revert to the mean, I somehow managed to miss every deadline I was given on this book, leading to scheduling conflicts, late night emails, and not one but two delays to the publication date.

So particular thanks for the loving patience and support of my long-time, long-suffering editor, Lizzie Henry, and to Reid Tracy, Michelle Pilley, Julie Oughton, Leanne Siu Anastasi, Margarete Nielsen, and the entire Hay House family for continuing to believe in me and never once deriding or pressuring me to go any faster than the creative force and I seemed to want to go.

If it's true that it takes a village to raise a child, it's equally true that it takes a team to bring a book into the world. Fortunately, I have a world-class one. On the book side, it all begins with my agent, Robert Kirby, who has somehow figured out that plying me with alcohol, good food, and great company stirs my creative juices. 'I'll know it when I see it' must be the single most annoying thing for a designer to hear, but Randy Stuart provided another brilliant cover design and continually provides multiple possibilities for my limited visual imagination to sift through.

On the Genius Catalyst side of things, infinite love and thanks to my business manager, Michelle 'I don't deserve you' Walder; my creative director, Lynne 'QOFE' Robertson; and my assistant, Annette 'Sparkles' Watling. Without these three dynamic, capable women at the helm, I would be awash with great ideas and nowhere to put them, and no way to share them with the world.

Particular thanks to some of the early readers on this project – Steve Chandler, Paul McKenna, Barb Patterson, George Pransky, and Peter Wright all took the time to wade through the muck of my early drafts and offer up their unique and valuable perspectives. The book and I are both very much the better for it.

Creating the Impossible has existed as an online program since 2009, so a heartfelt thank you goes to the thousands of participants who've joined in over the years and helped me clarify and refine the key principles that make the impossible possible. I've only shared a tiny number of your stories in this book, but your participation and willingness to get yourself out of the way for long enough to see that miracles do happen and dreams can come true is a constant inspiration to me.

Along those lines, special thanks to Kai Beeler, Robin Charbit, Ami Chen Mills-Naim, Bill Cumming, Don Donovan, Mara Gleason, Bill Goldstein, David Key, Sandy Krot, Ken Manning, Eirik Grunde Olsen, and Kaye Taylor for letting me share your stories. It is my fondest hope that your success in creating the impossible inspires countless others to do the same.

Five names to go…

To my best friend and 'first responder' for the past 30 years, David Beeler, I can't thank you enough. It's difficult to put a value on the depth of your friendship and utter willingness to listen as I put voice to my crazy ideas for the first time. It's amazing to me how many of those 'crazy ideas' have come to fruition, but more amazing still that you've always been there every step of the way.

To my gorgeous wife, Nina – all I can say is that I'm the luckiest man in the world to have gotten the chance to live with you for this long and to have somehow managed not to mess things up along the way. The idea that I get to love someone this much who loves me back as fiercely and with as much kindness, patience, and humor as you do would have been my impossible dream when we first met three decades ago.

And last, but by no means least, to our beautiful 'co-creations,' Oliver, Clara, and Maisy – you are my favorite things about being alive.

Permissions

Extract on p.24 reprinted with permission of the publisher. From *The Highest Goal*, copyright © 2005 by Professor Michael Ray, Berrett-Koehler Publishers, Inc., San Francisco, CA. All rights reserved. www.bkconnection.com

Extract on p.171 reprinted with permission of the publisher. From *The Art of Possibility* by Rosamund Stone Zander and Benjamin Zander. Harvard Business Press Books, 2000.

ABOUT THE AUTHOR

David Beeler

Michael Neill is an internationally renowned transformative coach and the best-selling author of *The Inside-Out Revolution*, *The Space Within*, *You Can Have What You Want*, *Supercoach*, and both the *Effortless Success* and *Coaching from the Inside-Out* self-study programs. He has spent more than 25 years as a coach, adviser, friend, mentor, and creative spark plug to celebrities, CEOs, royalty, and people who want to get more out of themselves and their lives. He is also the founder of **Supercoach Academy**, an international school that certifies coaches in the art and science of transformative coaching.

Michael's books have been translated into 18 languages, and his public talks, retreats and seminars have touched and transformed lives at the United Nations and on six continents. He hosts a weekly talk show on HayHouseRadio.com, and his weekly Caffeine for the Soul blogs and podcasts can be found at MichaelNeill.org. His TEDx talk, 'Why Aren't We Awesomer?', has been viewed by nearly 200,000 people around the world.

You can follow him on Facebook and Twitter:

f mneill

🐦 @michael_neill

www.MichaelNeill.org

We hope you enjoyed this Hay House book. If you'd like to receive our online catalog featuring additional information on Hay House books and products, or if you'd like to find out more about the Hay Foundation, please contact:

Hay House, Inc., P.O. Box 5100, Carlsbad, CA 92018-5100
(760) 431-7695 or (800) 654-5126
(760) 431-6948 (fax) or (800) 650-5115 (fax)
www.hayhouse.com® • www.hayfoundation.org

———

Published and distributed in Australia by:
Hay House Australia Pty. Ltd., 18/36 Ralph St., Alexandria NSW 2015
Phone: 612-9669-4299 • *Fax:* 612-9669-4144 • www.hayhouse.com.au

Published and distributed in the United Kingdom by:
Hay House UK, Ltd., Astley House, 33 Notting Hill Gate, London W11 3JQ
Phone: 44-20-3675-2450 • *Fax:* 44-20-3675-2451 • www.hayhouse.co.uk

Published in India by: Hay House Publishers India,
Muskaan Complex, Plot No. 3, B-2, Vasant Kunj, New Delhi 110 070
Phone: 91-11-4176-1620 • *Fax:* 91-11-4176-1630 • www.hayhouse.co.in

Distributed in Canada by:
Raincoast Books, 2440 Viking Way, Richmond, B.C. V6V 1N2
Phone: 1-800-663-5714 • *Fax:* 1-800-565-3770 • www.raincoast.com

———

Access New Knowledge.
Anytime. Anywhere.

Learn and evolve at your own pace
with the world's leading experts.

www.hayhouseU.com